BE A BETTER LEADER NOW!

New Insights on
10 Powerful Skills that Will
Dramatically Increase Your
Leadership Effectiveness

Kirk Wilkinson

Be a Better Leader NOW!
New Insights on 10 Powerful Skills
that Will Dramatically Increase Your
Leadership Effectiveness
Published by Transformational
Insights International, 2016
Mesa, Arizona

Copyright © 2016 by Kirk Wilkinson

All rights reserved

Includes bibliographical references

ISBN 978-1-943784-72-1

Cover design by Susan Veach
Edited by Erin Martineau

Dedicated to my father
Ron Wilkinson
1938 – 2014

Contents

"Kirk is the most motivational, inspirational and life changing coach I have ever had both personally and professionally. His insights, instincts and ability to communicate and interpret, bring even the best of groups closer and more effective."

Talia Brott - *Sales Manager - eSignLive*

"As a client of Kirk's, I am thrilled that he has written a book just for leaders. I was fortunate to have Kirk personally help me develop many of my natural leadership skills using several of the tools in this book. I have since gone on in my career to be named "Leader of the Year" at my workplace, as well as managing a leadership development program within my company. This book is like having several one-on-one sessions with Kirk, allowing the reader to hone-in on the skills that need development, or reinforce those talents already in practice. I highly recommend this book (and Kirk as a coach) to all who lead, aspire to lead, or just want to improve their interpersonal skills in general."

Alison Brooks, *Marketing Manager,*
Destination Hotels

"For the past 6 years Kirk has played a significant role in our innovative leadership development program. Our rising stars often site the one on one coaching with Kirk as the most valued aspect of the program. He is an incredible listener and imparts his wisdom through a few meaningful nuggets that inspire improvement."

Greg Miller – *Destination Hotels – Vice President and*
Area Managing Director

"Kirk Wilkinson has an uncanny ability to read people and not only create an awareness of one's natural gifts, talents and strengths but learn to hone them in such a way that success is inevitable. In my coaching sessions with Kirk, he dove right into determining what made me tick. He quickly began to uncover my natural gifts, and helped me understand how they impacted both my professional and personal life. Kirk also teaches you that your gifts can be perceived in different ways, so he offers insight into how to tune them in and tune them out as needed."

Carrie McKeever – *Assistant Director of Catering Services, Sanctuary Camelback Mountain Resort and Spa*

Introduction

You can be a better leader starting right now! Whether you are a seasoned executive, recently promoted to management, or an aspiring leader or manager, this book is for you. Perhaps you feel you need a leadership 'tune-up' or received critical feedback in your performance evaluation. Maybe you want to start off on the right foot as a new manager. Whatever your motivation is for picking up this book, it will help you become a better leader.

This is a 'how-to' book, but it is not a step-by-step instruction manual on leadership or a daily script to follow. My purpose is to provide new insights on real-world practical skills that arise from leadership principles that are proven and timeless. I would like you to think of this book as a roadmap or blueprint for exceptional leadership. There is a lot of material available on *what* to do, and I want to help you learn *how* to do it – how to Be a Better Leader NOW!

The world needs better leaders! During my 40 years of employment, I have really only had one job that I would consider a "bad" job. However, I have had my share of bad managers. Sadly, I get the same report from most of my clients. Early in my career at Hewlett Packard (HP), after having the same position as a Systems Engineer for six years, I began to hate my job. It was surprising to me to discover that I began hating my job because I had worked very hard to get hired by HP and had been satisfied with my job and my pay for some time.

But almost overnight I began to have strong feelings of dissatisfaction to the point that I began to look for a new job with another company. During the process of looking for a new job, the team was reorganized, and I ended up reporting to a different manager. Things improved. I quickly realized that I didn't hate my job; I disliked my former manager. And with the reorganization, my job satisfaction returned. There are more bad managers than there are bad jobs.

When I ask my clients to think of the best manager they have worked for, I rarely hear people talk about their current manager. Typically, it is a manager they had in the beginning of their career, someone who took time to nurture them and demonstrate interest in them. This begs the question, "Where are all the good managers?" It seems that there are no better managers now than when I first started my career. Sure, you could blame the economy, or downsizing, or some other external factor, but I believe the answer is more intrinsic.

Over the past several decades, the amount of information on how to be a good leader has grown exponentially. A recent search on Amazon.com for books on leadership returned more than 95,000 books. Refining the search to only hardcopy books to eliminate duplications resulted yet in a staggering 65,000 titles! And that is just in books! With all the material on how to be a good leader in books, videos, online content, and face-to-face training, you would think that there would be more good managers and leaders now than at any other time in history.

Sadly, that is just not the case. Good managers and great leaders are as rare now as they were 40 years ago. Some would even say that good managers are more rare now than they were then. Again, it begs the question, "Where are all the good leaders?"

Over the past 25 years that I have been giving seminars and coaching executives and individuals, I have asked the questions: what makes a great leader or manager? The most common responses suggest that great leaders and managers are:

- creative
- visionary
- charismatic
- ambitious
- luckier
- great communicators
- risk-takers

- caring
- heroic
- prone to make big, bold moves
- extroverted
- intelligent
- experienced

A similar list can be found in the book *Great by Choice* by Jim Collins (Collins & Hansen, 2011). In his book, Jim Collins points out that, yes, great leaders have these qualities; yet, so do their "not-so-great" peers. That, too, has been my experience. Sure, many great leaders are charismatic, visionary, and great communicators; but those characteristics and the others listed above are not what determines greatness because bad leaders and not-so-great managers share those same characteristics. And sometimes the best leaders can even be introverted people. How, then, can poor leaders become great? How can a bad manager become a good, and perhaps even great, manager?

I try to answer that question in this book by sharing with you the skills and concepts I have used successfully with hundreds of clients and thousands of individuals in workshops around the globe. Since December 1990, I have been fortunate to spend more than 2,500 hours in one-on-one interviews with executives and small business owners and have logged more than 6,000 hours coaching executives, managers, and individuals. Those interviews combined with my own observations, coaching sessions with individuals, and my own personal experiences are the basis for this book on how to *Be a Better Leader Now!*

This is a book for anyone who is currently a leader or manager or would like to become one. It is a book about force multipliers. A force multiplier can be defined as a factor that dramatically increases (and, thus, "multiplies") the effectiveness of an item or group. Each section in this book is a force multiplier! As you apply the concepts, skills, and methods in this book, your effectiveness as a leader will be multiplied and will positively impact the people with whom you work. And more importantly, it will increase the effectiveness of all that you do.

I have witnessed great leaders who would not be considered great communicators, as well as great managers who weren't all that creative. At the same time, I have seen individuals pass up lucrative promotions to continue to work for a manager who was not charismatic or all that experienced. No matter what you bring to the table, the skills in this book will make a significant difference by enhancing and expanding your already-great characteristics.

All too often someone becomes a manager because they have done a good job as an individual contributor. He or she is thrust into a leadership position with little or no training on how to lead. Their effectiveness is left up to chance, trial, and error. Why take a chance on your abilities as a leader? This book will help you take a more proactive and architected approach to being a leader; in other words, it will give you the skills to multiply your effectiveness – to become a *better* leader!

Before I go on, however, let me provide a disclaimer. If you expect a scientific journal that reports on research studies with charts, graphs, and empirical data, then this book is not for you. There are already plenty of books like that. If you are looking for a fluffy book with all the hype about merely having a positive attitude and being an energetic leader, then this is not the book you need. This is a 'how to' book based on observation and experience presented in a conversational tone with stories and practical skills that can be implemented immediately.

There is no need to read this book sequentially, as it is intended that each section stand on its own. However, I have done my best to put the concepts in order of importance and impact, as well as in logical order. My only recommendation is that you begin with the section on trust, as it sets the tone and foundation for all other sections in this book. Another disclaimer is that there is no magic bullet in this book. All of the concepts I present are tried and true but take serious consideration and work to implement.

You don't need to give up who you are to be a great leader. This book is about multiplying the effectiveness of your leadership and management, not by throwing out all that you have learned and have been doing, but by

maximizing the return on those things through the introduction of powerful real-world concepts and skills that
really work. Each of the concepts and skills in this book
will multiply your return on investment. They will enhance
your ability to lead and manage.

As a bonus, these same skills and concepts will help
you improve every aspect of your life. These concepts are
not only for the workplace but also for your personal life
and relationships. The goal is for you to become great by
adding the skills covered in this book to your natural talents and gifts. My hope is that you will take these skills as
I present them and consider them deeply, ponder and practice them, and internalize them so that you can become a
better leader now!

Interestingly, the list of skills that are force multipliers
for leadership is not an exhaustive list, and I have deliberately included only a bare minimum in this book. In my
coaching program, I cover more than seventeen skills and
concepts. In this book, however, I focus on the top ten in
order to keep the book somewhat short and readily accessible, to-the-point, and easy to read. The skills, concepts,
and approaches included here are the result of real-world
application with people who have had the courage to take
action and have achieved amazing results.

As a coach I am often brought in as a last resort to help
"save" a manager's or executive's job. The skills in this book
are what I have used to help these individuals transform
poor performance into top performance. I am fortunate to
have more than a 96% success rate with my coaching clients, measured by how many executives and managers I
have coached who have overcome their limiting attitudes

and behaviors in order to retain their jobs, become better leaders, and rise to their peak performance.

The skills covered in this book have not only helped poor performing managers become top performers; they will also help any executive or manager become a better leader. This book will also help you as a manager or leader to assist those who aspire to become a manager or leader. With the guidance you obtain in this book, you will be able to help others become better leaders than they would become otherwise. These skills and concepts in this book have all been tried and tested in the field with surprising results. Here are the skills covered:

1. The Trust Advantage
2. The Optimist's Advantage
3. It's All About the WHO
4. The Art of Appreciation
5. Context, Context, Context
6. The Art of Disclaimers
7. Authentic Curiosity
8. Confident Humility
9. Discipline and Deferred Gratification
10. The Art of Macro-Management

The ten skills above have been organized into a roadmap to help you become a better leader. Again, it is not necessary that you read them in order. Each chapter (skill) has been written to stand on its own. However, the skills are arranged so that they build upon and reinforce each other.

The power and effectiveness of these skills will come by learning and implementing them in order. For example, the Art of Macro-Management is much more effective after building trust, becoming more optimistic, and demonstrating confident humility. As you read this book you will notice a natural overlap of skills, concepts, and topics. This is deliberate, as they are ordered and designed to support one another.

It is my intention to write this book in a conversational tone, as if we were sitting together in a coaching session one-on-one. The purpose for this is to make these concepts readily accessible to leaders and managers in every field and to those who want to become leaders.

Chapter 1

The Trust Advantage

In Latin there is a term, Sine Qua Non, that translated literally means "without which no"; meaning that without this one ingredient, this one important thing, the outcome, wish, or result that is desired or expected cannot be accomplished.

When presenting to a group, I often ask what the Sine Qua Non of leadership is? The common answers include integrity, consistency, communication, heart, confidence, accountability, and many of the same traits outlined in the introduction. There are so many traits and qualities that make a good manager, you could spend the rest of your career focusing on a new trait every month and still not exhaust the list for many years.

However, even if you did that and gave it all you had, you may still come up short if you don't start with the real Sine Qua Non of leadership – in other words, the one thing necessary for effective leadership. When missing, all other great leadership traits and management skills are undermined and will never be adequate. Leadership cannot result in enduring success and optimal effectiveness without this one thing.

That one thing is trust. Trust is the Sine Qua Non of Leadership. In his book *The Speed of Trust*, Stephen M. R. Covey makes this same point on the very first page: "There is one thing that is common to every individual, relationship, team, family, organization, nation, economy, and civilization throughout the world – one thing which, if removed, will destroy the most powerful government, the most successful business, the most thriving economy, the most influential leadership, the greatest friendship, the strongest character, the deepest love...that one thing is trust" (Covey, 2006).

Great leaders know this, but what even great leaders may not understand is that trust is a skill; and like most skills, it can be taught, learned, and developed. Trust is the single most important of the force multipliers of leadership. There is no amount of leadership style, charisma, communication, or pizzazz that can overcome a lack of trust.

More than 90% of the executives whom I have interviewed and coached have indicated that a lack of trust was the number-one problematic issue among their senior leaders. The same is true for the multitude of first level managers with whom I have worked. Lack of trust is singularly the greatest cause of failure in organizations. Robert F. Hurley reported in the Harvard Business Review that roughly half of all managers don't trust their leaders (Hurley, 2006).

Hurley goes on to cite a University of Chicago study, which reported that more than 4 out of 5 Americans have little trust in the people running corporations. Another study reported in the Harvard Business Review showed that 58% of employees would trust a stranger more than they trust their boss (Segalla, 2009). In the same report employees indicated that they would choose a better boss over a raise.

This is reversible! It can be overcome! Even if trust is lost, it can be rebuilt. Certainly, the greater the lack of trust, the harder it will be to rebuild trust; but it can be done, and with the skills I am about to share with you, it can be done much faster and more effectively than you may think. Trust is personal. It is a deep-seated emotion. To trust someone requires you to be vulnerable because trusting requires taking a risk – a risk that a person, a company, or a product will betray that trust. Trust is vital to every relationship.

When the topic of trust comes up, we most often think about interpersonal trust. There are other forms of trust that are just as important, but all forms of it have their basis and foundation in interpersonal trust. For instance, if someone feels betrayed by a product brand, it is likely that they will take it personally. Let's say that someone has purchased a certain brand of car over and over again, and the car purchased most recently does not live up to their previous standard of trust. They will feel personally betrayed by the brand and the car company.

A perfect example of this is the experience of my good friend Anna. Anna spent a significant amount of time researching her next car purchase. She settled on a Volkswagen Pasatt. Her primary criteria of Volkswagen and the Passatt was her concern for the environment. Based on her research, the Volkswagen came out on top. Not long after her purchase, the news broke regarding the scam and deception of Volkswagen falsifying their emissions data. Anna felt personally betrayed. She had given her trust to Volkswagen, and even though it involved something as impersonal as a car, the breach of trust was personal to her.

The same is true for organizations. As a leader you may be distrusted by no fault of your own, if your employees do not trust upper management or the corporation. However, regardless of the source of mistrust, as a leader you can manage it and overcome it. In my book *The TRUST Advantage*, I elaborate on various types of trust, such as:

- Interpersonal Trust
- Self-Trust
- Organizational Trust
- Corporate Trust

I don't have room in this book to elaborate on all the aspects of trust but will focus on the practical side of trust: the *how-to* aspects of creating and rebuilding trust, as well as overcoming mistrust.

Trust is always personal. We most often think about interpersonal trust as the trust between two or more people. For example, if you were to say, "I don't trust John," you are most likely referring to this concept of interpersonal trust. However, one of the most important forms of trust is self-trust. This is significantly personal because, to the degree that you are able to trust yourself, you will be able to trust others.

Self-trust is demonstrated in such things as self-control, self-discipline, and confidence. Our ability to trust ourselves creates the sense in others that they can trust us. In other words, it adds to our trustworthiness. Without some level of self-trust, trusting others may be difficult. For example, if someone has been repeatedly rejected in their life, they may find it very difficult to trust others. They may have what we would call "trust issues." Have you ever met anyone with trust issues? People with trust issues believe that the real issue is interpersonal trust because they can't trust others. But what is actually happening lies within the combination of self-trust and interpersonal trust.

There are also aspects of trust on the professional side, such as organizational trust. As an employee, do you trust your organization? If you are a manager or supervisor, organizational trust is very important because you may get the blame for a lack of trust an employee has in the overall organization. Or it could be that your employees don't trust senior leadership, the quality of the product or services produced by your company, or even the policies and programs. This is what is known as corporate trust.

Corporate trust will be reflected in how your employees respond on employee surveys, where you receive low marks based on employees' lack of trust in the top executives. Corporate trust can suffer when employees don't believe in the quality of the product. For example, let's say that customers report that your company's products or services don't meet the customer's standard of quality and nothing is done about it. This can cause employees to lose faith in the products and the company, which affects corporate trust. Corporate mistrust diminishes your organizational trust. As your organizational trust diminishes, you begin to mistrust the people to whom you report on an interpersonal basis, and you may find yourself stuck in a job you don't like. Soon it starts to affect your own self-trust.

These four aspects of trust come together to create a trust matrix. When I refer to trust throughout the remainder of this section, I refer to it in the context of all four forms of trust: corporate, organizational, interpersonal trust, and self-trust. However, I will focus mostly on interpersonal trust and self-trust, which I believe are the foundation for all the other forms of trust.

The Trust Advantage

Trust, when learned and applied, creates an advantage. Not only does it create a personal competitive advantage, it creates a corporate advantage on the business side, as well. From a business perspective there are at least two things that happen when trust increases. The first might be obvious. As trust increases, so does employee engagement and satisfaction.

The second upside is prosperity or profitability. Companies that rate high on trust actually do better financially. Employee engagement, creativity, and performance all go up. Subsequently, costs, blame, and resentment go down. Skepticism, gossiping, and rumors also decrease.

Learning the skill of trust and implementing it gives you and your company an advantage with some very tangible benefits. In 2002, a competitive services market survey was performed with Holiday Inn (Simons, 2002). One of the questions on the survey was, "Does my manager deliver on promises?" I want you to think for a minute how you would answer that question. Does your manager deliver on promises?

Those of you who have taken employee surveys before know there is always a question like this, and Holiday Inn had this among many questions in their employee survey of 6,500 employees from 76 hotels. They later correlated the results of that one question to the profit of the hotels. They found that the higher the behavioral integrity of the managers, the higher the profit. Further analysis showed that a

1/8 improvement in the score showed a 2.5 percent increase in profit, representing an increased average of $250,000 per hotel.

The survey found that no other single aspect of a manager's behavior had this kind of an impact on the bottom line. In fact, they actually found that there was no other aspect to their business that had such an impact on profit. When they looked at marketing impact, salary impact, and employee satisfaction overall, none of it had the same impact on profit as that small change in the score for manager behavior relating to trust. Imagine! 1/8 improvement equates to a 2.5 percent difference in profit. Now, I want you to calculate the difference 2.5% profit growth would make at your company or organization!

Trust has far-reaching implications. Increased trust results in increased morale, motivation, retention, and employee satisfaction. The beauty is that not only does it affect the bottom line, it it has ancillary benefits as lower costs and interestingly enough, the number of employee sick days decreases. When employees are healthier, have less stress, are motivated and engaged, you will find that they will learn what costs are being wasted without you having to do cost-cutting measures. They will feel that they can come forward with an idea that will make a difference because creativity and innovation go up.

So the real question is this: if this is true, why is the behavioral integrity of managers so difficult to develop? Why is trust so hard to obtain or maintain? The answer represents factors that need to be addressed and overcome. Within an organization, developing and maintaining trust is difficult because of the various ways that mistrust can be created through the following:

- Unclear or often-changing priorities
- Competing stakeholders
- Shifting policies
- Cost cutting
- Attrition of good people
- Changing markets and economic conditions

As a leader, the better you are at handling the issues that create mistrust, the better you will be at establishing a culture of trust. It comes down to this: how can you teach, train, or learn behavioral integrity and develop trust? The answer lies below in the TRUST Formula for learning, teaching, and developing trust that will result in an overall culture of trust and create a competitive advantage – both a personal and organizational competitive advantage.

The TRUST Formula

We all strive to be trusted. And it can be difficult, even painful, to hear that we may not be trusted. Prior to my first meeting with Randy, I met with the division general manager to whom Randy reported. The general manager shared that he didn't trust Randy and gave me many examples of how Randy had lost his trust. Randy was devastated to hear that his boss and others didn't trust him. For the most part, Randy was unaware.

Fortunately, he was willing to learn the formula I am about to share with you. The formula to rebuild trust is the same, regardless of how trust has been lost or compromised. The formula to overcoming the mistrust of a team is the same as the formula to regaining trust that has been lost by the betrayal of a loved one.

Even when it is not your fault, as a leader or manager it is your responsibility to build, rebuild, or regain trust when it has been underdeveloped, broken, or lost, just like it is the responsibility of the betrayer to regain the trust of those who have been betrayed. To do this, use what I call the TRUST formula. It is simple in concept and yet powerful in its application. The TRUST formula is this:

T: Trustworthy – Take steps and actions to become more worthy of someone's trust.

R: Responsibility – Being responsible and accountable are a critical aspect of trust.

U: Under-React – Learning not to freak out or overreact builds trust.

S: Sincerity – Being sincere and having the highest integrity is a key component of trust.

T: Transparency – There must be no hidden agendas and no strings attached.

This is a proven formula that works for teams and individuals alike. The application in a team setting may differ from the application on a personal level. But the formula has been proven to help rebuild trust. Let's examine the formula more closely.

T: Trustworthy - Take steps and actions to become more worthy of someone's trust.

Learn to Trust Yourself

Let me reiterate that trust is personal. It is one of the most personal things we have, that we give, and that we feel and experience every single day and sometimes every single minute of our lives. It is deeply personal. If you don't believe me, think of a time when your trust has been abused, taken, or betrayed. How do you feel? Bad? What kind of bad? Devastated, hurt, offended, broken? Don't those sound like personal feelings?

The personal nature of trust arises from how we feel about and perceive ourselves. People who have high-self worth – those who feel good about themselves and have a positive perception of themselves – are easier to trust and to be trusted. Those who suffer from a diminished sense of self-worth and, thus, low self-esteem and poor self-confidence, will likely find it harder to trust others. And it is harder for us to trust them.

Self-worth not only has a lot to do with trust and how you trust, it is also a key determining factor in your personal level of happiness, satisfaction, and optimism. Your self-worth, self-esteem, and self-confidence have bearing on your ability to be a better leader. Rather than take the time here to discuss self-worth and how you can improve it, I have included a bonus section on that topic at the end of this book. I highly recommend that you take a few minutes and read that section to see how you can improve your personal life, leadership, and ability to trust yourself and others by improving your self-worth.

Perhaps someone has come to mind while you are reading this, and you think to yourself, *I find it really hard to trust that person*. There's a good chance that the reason that you find it hard to trust them is either because they suffer from low self-esteem, or you do. If it's not you, then it's them. If it's not them, then it's you. Again, trust is very personal.

When it comes to trust, it is logical and natural to think that trust is solely dependent on the actions of the other person. In other words, you will trust them as long as they behave appropriately and don't do anything to betray your trust. But, as I have described, our ability, willingness, and desire to trust others stems from how we feel about ourselves. So if you want to have confidence in giving your trust to others, it is important to recognize how you feel about yourself – whether you consider yourself 'worthy' of someone's trust – and that includes trusting yourself. Becoming more trustworthy begins with learning to trust yourself, which includes trusting in your judgment, intuition, ideas, abilities, skills, natural gifts, and talents. It also means trusting that you will do what is right, even when things get hard.

Let me share this example of self-trust. When Sam first started working for me, I immediately noticed he had trust issues. He had corporate conspiracy theories, felt that top management was out to get him, and would continually second-guess decisions and direction. Sam spent a lot of time and energy managing his mistrust to the point that it was impacting his performance. I worked hard to build trust with Sam by using the skills I am sharing with you in this book.

After some time, Sam confided in me that he was a struggling cocaine addict and had recently celebrated one year of sobriety. Sam explained how hard it had been for him to cover up his addiction. He also struggled to hide feelings of guilt and low self-worth. As I listened to Sam, I understood more about his trust issues. It was hard for him to trust others because he was living a double life – that of an addict and that of a senior professional on my team.

Over the months that followed I saw a dramatic change in Sam. The longer he was clean and sober, the

more trusting he became. I do not mean to say that everyone with an addiction will have trust issues; that is not the
point. The point is that Sam found it difficult to trust himself. And that lack of trust was projected onto others.

One more thought regarding self-trust; there's almost
an aura around us that tells people whether or not we can
be trusted. Have you ever met someone for the first time
and within the first 30 seconds you know whether or not
you can trust them? You sense it in their words, body language, and demeanor. It's quite likely that it is related to
their level of self-trust.

By learning how to trust yourself more, you also
become more worthy of others' trust in you. In my book *I
AM STRONG – The Formula to Build your Self-Worth*, I go
into detail on how to get to know yourself so that you can
trust yourself more. I won't repeat that here, but know that
as you learn to trust yourself more, you can then be more
trusting of others; and, in turn, you become more trustworthy yourself. Following are the skills that you can practice to improve your self-trust and create a higher degree
of trustworthiness.

Demonstrate Loyalty

Another aspect of becoming trustworthy is learning to
demonstrate trust in others and loyalty. Former CEO of
Johnson & Johnson Jim Burke said, "I found that by trusting people until they prove themselves unworthy of trust,
a lot more happens" (Covey, 2006). How can you demonstrate trust in others?

We demonstrate loyalty by both our actions and
words. Let me give you some words to use in any situation
that I consider magic words, particularly for supervisors,

managers, and executives. Someone comes to you with a question, problem, or issue, or it could simply be a conversation. You can demonstrate loyalty and therefore trust by asking something like this, "What do you think?" Then zip your lip and wait until it becomes uncomfortable – uncomfortable enough for the other person to know you are serious.

"What do you think?" are magic words, not because of their literal meaning, but because of the message it sends. You could also try these magic words: "Hmm that's very interesting. Tell me, what you would do?" Another magic phrase is this: "You know what? I really don't have an opinion about this. I trust you to do the right thing, to make the right choice, and to work it out. I'm here for you if you need me." These are very powerful phrases that work with children, spouses and partners, clients, employees, and managers.

Personally, I love it when someone says to me, "Well, what do you think?" Or when someone says, "I trust you to do the right thing, so I'm not really going to worry about it because I know it's in good hands." Imagine how you would feel if your boss or manager were to say that to you. It truly is powerful.

My recommendation is to begin to use phrases like these that convey loyalty, even if you don't feel it 100%. Several years ago I inherited several employees to my team. These employees came from various organizations and all had different backgrounds. In one of my first meetings with Jason, he told me of a complicated and bothersome issue with one the partners that he managed.

I listened, acknowledged the situation and the complexity, and then said, "It seems you have given this a lot of thought, and I trust your judgment. Do what you think is best, and I will back you up." Though Jason was new to my team, he had studied the issue and seemed to be able to handle it. So I felt showing loyalty was more important than giving my opinion.

His jaw dropped, and he asked if I was sure. I was sure, and I told him so. That one short conversation set the tone and basis for a long and productive relationship with Jason. He became a top performer on my team. Even years later when I ran into him at a social event, he mentioned that first conversation. Demonstrating loyalty really works.

Another way to demonstrate loyalty is by demonstrating that you have someone's back. Early on in my career I made the decision to terminate an employee because I believed it was the right thing to do given the circumstances. Many of my stakeholders thought that it was the worst decision I could have made. The decision to terminate a well-liked employee created quite a stir, and my manager was feeling the heat, as well. One day my manager took me aside and said, "Kirk, your decision has turned into a terrible situation, very political, and a lot people are upset. But I want you to know that I've got your back."

Wow! I felt his loyalty, and in that moment he became more worthy of my trust. He became trustworthy, and it meant a lot to me. I thought that I was going to get fired for doing the right thing, and he was loyal to me by expressing that he had my back. When someone says that to you, what do you give in return? You give them your trust.

You might be surprised at how many people walk around with an intense feeling that no one has their back. I ask most of my clients who has their back in their personal lives and at work. Most of the time the answer is, "I don't know." By demonstrating loyalty, that you have someone's back, you generate feelings of trust – you become trust-worthy.

Be Predictable

The more predictable you are, the more trustworthy you become. That is not to say that you have to give up being spontaneous or extemporaneous. It comes down to whether people can count on you to act, react, talk, and perform in a predictable fashion that is consistent with what they consider good character.

However, you don't necessarily have to like someone to trust them. Recently, I was asked to coach a finance manager who had the reputation for being mean and uncooperative. As I interviewed his stakeholders, they all indicated that although Jerry, the finance manager, was mean, disrespect-ful, and often-times harsh, they trusted his finance judg-ment. When I probed further, I found that because Jerry was predictably mean, they knew how to deal with him. And because his finance judgment was sound, consistent, and trustworthy, he was valued in spite of his crankiness.

I find this quite interesting because if someone is a jerk and their misbehavior is predictable, they may garner more trust than a person whose poor behavior is unpredictable. When it comes to being worthy of trust, being consistent and predictable is an important way to build trust and keep it. Don't get me wrong. This is not meant as permission to be mean or be a jerk. It is an example of being predictable.

Being predictable is a good way to demonstrate that people can trust you. Keep in mind that being predictable does not mean you have to be boring or weak. Being pre-dictable does not mean you don't take risks or innovate. It simply means that people want to understand how you will react in certain situations. Being predictable builds trust.

In much of the literature on predictability and trust, predictability is discussed in terms of being consistent. When people see you acting in a consistent manner, they are more willing to extend their trust. Consistency also has other benefits. For example, I am a big fan of In-N-Out Burger. Established in Southern California in the late 1940s, In-N-Out is a model of consistency and quality. No matter what location you visit, you will experience the same food quality, the same level of customer service, and the same menu. In-N-Out loyalists value the consistent quality.

Their consistency goes beyond the quality food, extending to everything they do. Each month (or "period," as In-N-Out employees call it), they do a deep cleaning of the entire building. They remove the grills, cover up all the paper goods, and scour the restaurant from top to bottom with a pressure washer. This also includes getting on the roof and pressure-washing the exhaust fans. As demonstrated by In-N-Out Burger, your personal predictability and consistency at offering high-quality products and services will generate trust, which will lead to higher profits.

We live in an uncertain world where, in many cases, predictability has been thrown out the window. In this ever-changing world it is even more important for you, as a leader, to be predictable and to use that consistency as a competitive advantage. When managers or leaders are continually changing direction and strategy, it creates mistrust and frustration in employees and clientele. People stop following those who are unpredictable or inconsistent because they don't want to invest their time and emotion in something that will just change anyway.

Even a small improvement in being predictable will foster greater trust. Consistency and predictability are built on the small things, and on the daily or frequent interactions with others. I know that for some of you, being predictable seems boring. I assure you, it is not. You can be very dynamic, fun, capable, and spontaneous and still leverage predictability as a pathway to greater trustworthiness.

Becoming more worthy of someone's trust is an important part of building and maintaining trust. However, like trust, the TRUST formula has many facets. Each part of the formula is important and should be considered together, as well as individually. Every part of the formula is about creating trustworthiness and should be considered in that context. The TRUST formula proceeds with R for Responsibility.

R: Responsibility – Being responsible and accountable are a critical aspect of trust.

What would be the best compliment anyone could give you? I ask this question of nearly all my clients, and among the most common answers is: "I trust you." Being trusted is a meaningful compliment. For many, it would be one of the best compliments they could receive.

Developing, building, and maintaining trust requires you to be responsible. Most of us know what it means to be responsible, and, rather than use some elaborate definition or send you to look it up in the dictionary, let me just use a simple explanation of what it means to be responsible. Being responsible, especially in the context of trust, simply means to make and keep promises.

This principle reminds me of the survey performed by Holiday Inn, where corporate leaders asked employees if their direct manager makes and keeps promises. Why is this question so important? People will trust you more when you demonstrate that you consistently do what you say you are going to do. That is the essence of responsibility.

When it comes to making and keeping promises, the smaller and more frequent the promises, the better. When I refer to a promise, I am referring to any implication that you will do something. It can be something as small as showing up on time for a meeting or arriving when you say you will. It might be something as simple as texting someone back and returning phone calls. All of those small and seemingly insignificant things are an implied promise and, as they are kept, trust increases.

You may be asking, "What about big promises?" It goes without saying that keeping big promises, such as to not steal from the company, to be faithful to a spouse or partner, or to obey the law, is expected and paramount. But in my work as a life coach working with couples, I have found that couples are more emotionally equipped to deal with and forgive big promises that are broken but have a harder time dealing with the small and petty promises that we make each and every day. Either way, trust is built on consistently practicing integrity and responsibility, which is the idea that if you say you are going to do something or if it is implied, then do it!

At the risk of stating the obvious, people who are perceived as being irresponsible are not as well trusted as those who take responsibility and integrity seriously. As a test of this concept, think about lending your car to a teenage driver who has received multiple speeding tickets and has had a few accidents. Most of us would be reluctant, if not unwilling altogether, to let them borrow a car.

Although we may be reluctant to lend our car to *any* teenager, it would be a bit easier if we knew that the teen was a responsible driver. Our culture and society reward responsibility. Responsible drivers have lower insurance rates, for example. Responsible employees are paid more and given better assignments. If you want people to trust you more, then be responsible.

In a recent coaching session, a client said, "I don't trust John at all!" She said this with such emotion that I immediately sensed the betrayal she felt. John was her direct manager and an executive at her company. I knew John and felt I could trust him, so I was naturally curious as to why she felt she couldn't trust John.

Here is what she told me. In the previous year she had several conversations with John about a pending promotion and the corresponding pay increase. In her story, John had committed to giving her the promotion at the beginning of the new fiscal year. But the fiscal year began with no promotion. After several weeks, she approached John about the promised promotion. He told her that it was not going to happen due to budget constraints and other priorities. She felt betrayed and, therefore, became unwilling to extend trust to John.

No matter what John had actually said, there was an implied promise to my client that she would get a promotion and the accompanying raise. You may look at this and fault John for promising or implying this if he couldn't or had no intention to follow through. Even so, John didn't do what he said he would do. He was irresponsible and, because of it, lost trust.

This kind of situation happens all the time in companies around the world where implied promises are not kept and trust is diminished. In this case, however, even without giving my client the promotion John could have turned this situation around and gained trust and respect be being more accountable. Following are some skills that you can practice in order to increase your responsibility, as well as the trust given to you from others.

Be Accountable

A close cousin to responsibility is accountability. Although they are synonymous, in the context of trust, they are worth addressing separately. Where responsibility is about making and keeping promises, accountability is owning your actions, your behavior, and the outcome, whether you have kept your promises or not.

A manager who owns his mistakes and acknowledges them will be trusted more than one who does not. In the example above, John could have built trust by going to my client as soon as he knew she would not be able to get the promotion. If he had owned up to his commitment and inability to grant the promotion, he would likely have maintained her trust, in spite of her disappointment.

When we own up to our mistakes and acknowledge our implied promises, we build or maintain trust, even when things go wrong. I was recently checking into my room at the Gaylord Resort in Grapevine, Texas. I couldn't help overhearing another guest complaining about a mechanical noise in her room. As I watched the person at the front desk handle this, I saw accountability in action. The woman behind the desk listened intently, did not make excuses, and was apologetic while validating the complaint. Then she said this: "I will own this for you and make sure this is fixed. However, let me offer you another room and give you any assistance you will need to move your things."

The noise in the room was not the front desk clerk's problem. It was an engineering problem. But she was a responsible person. She chose to make herself accountable for solving the problem. By owning it and offering a solution with which the guest would be satisfied, the clerk increased trust and maintained customer satisfaction and loyalty. It is possible that the clerk had a manager who demonstrated responsibility and accountability. Managers who do this promote similar values and behaviors in their employees.

Owning mistakes and resolving them builds trust. Saying that leaders need to take responsibility for and admit their mistakes obviously implies that all leaders will or have made mistakes. This is true. Every brilliant, successful leader has erred. Understand that *you don't have to be perfect to be a better leader*. This is such an important part of building and maintaining a high degree of trustworthiness. It is ok, and I would say, important that you make mistakes. Not on purpose, mind you. But as a regular course of action, if you are afraid of making a mistake and are, therefore, super cautious, your team will sense that you don't trust yourself and will be reluctant to give you their full trust.

Making mistakes and then owning them is a real demonstration of accountability. Now, let me be clear; you don't have to throw yourself under the bus to own your mistakes. You don't need to continually fall on your sword to own your mistakes. You can own your mistakes in a professional and dignified manner. Of course, if you are continually having to own up to mistakes, there may be a bigger issue at hand related to responsibility that you will need to address. But when the occasional mistakes do happen, you can say, "I misjudged on that decision. I'm sorry. Here's how I will correct the situation..." This is how you demonstrate accountability.

Beyond owning your mistakes, accountability also includes owning your actions and behavior. We live in a world where it is very easy to justify just about any action and behavior. Also, throwing other people under the bus is the order of the day. To gain the trust of others is to refrain from justifying your poor behavior and blaming others. If you lead a team and your team missed a deadline or milestone, be accountable to your team by stepping up and owning it. You will increase the trust from your team and from other stakeholders.

Being accountable, however, has a dark side. Many managers and executives overuse accountability by owning things that don't belong to them. I have met many people whom I would consider to have the gift of exercising accountability as one of their core strengths. Perhaps you are one of those people who are able to own a project, a problem, or an issue and see it through.

If so, you may inadvertently gravitate toward owning things that don't belong to you. For example, you may neglect to delegate. But understand that you establish trust by owning less and letting others own important and significant things such as projects, tasks, ideas, and initiatives. Giving an employee an assignment that you consider important and significant demonstrates trust and gives them a chance to become accountable, as well.

Being accountable, owning what you should own, owning up to your mistakes and letting others be accountable builds trust. Be sure to own what you should own to avoid the danger of being perceived as incompetent.

Be Competent

Any discussion on trust and responsibility would be incomplete if it did not include the subject of competency. In many cases executives are promoted to leadership positions because they were good managers or individual contributors. In other words, they were promoted because they were competent. To build and maintain trust, it is imperative that you are competent; in other words, that you are able to do the job you have been hired to do.

Being competent doesn't mean you must know everything or have all the answers. It means that you are able to get the job done. All too often I hear complaints from employees who tell me their manager is "dumb" or has no clue about what the job entails. Not that long ago I was working with a client who serviced medical equipment as a field engineer. His team recently went through a reorganization, and his new boss came from the accounting department and had never worked in the field before. This new boss had no knowledge of the factors and issues that the field engineers faced each day. Subsequently, she was perceived as incompetent, and it created tremendous mistrust.

Employees don't trust someone who doesn't know what needs to be done and is unable to do it. When I facilitate a team meeting I am often surprised at how few people can answer the question, "What do you get paid to do?" As a manager or executive, you become a better leader and gain trust by becoming competent at your job and knowledgeable about or competent in what your employees get paid to do.

The good news is that competency is easily overcome through study and hard work to acquire the knowledge, skills, and experience necessary to succeed and excel. Competency combined with responsibility and accountability is powerful. Competency, responsibility, and accountability are prerequisite to building and maintaining trust. Together they complete the R: Responsibility component of the TRUST formula.

U: Under-React – Learning not to freak out or overreact builds trust.

Under-reacting is the opposite of "freaking-out." You may wonder why it is included here as part of the TRUST formula to build and maintain trust. An important aspect of trust is that people will find it hard to completely trust you if you overreact. If you have a tendency to freak out or blow up, people will not trust you with the truth. Why would they, if they believe that telling you the whole story will cause you to overreact? Instead, they will adjust the story, or refrain from telling the real story, or will keep things from you. If you want to be trusted, if you want to know the truth and the whole story, then it is critical that you learn to under-react.

Sure, you may say that under-reacting is a cop-out because there are some serious things that happen that require a bold response. Don't confuse under-reacting with a lack of strength. Think of under-reacting as the antidote to overreaction. Overreacting ultimately keeps you from finding the truth and can prevent you from coming up with the best resolution to a problem or challenge. When I have overreacted, I have been blinded by emotion and feelings that keep me from making the best assessments, responses, and decisions. It often prevents me from taking the time to listen and really hear.

Also, don't confuse under-reacting with apathy. Under-reacting doesn't mean you don't care or act unconcerned. It certainly doesn't mean you don't respond at all. It means approaching serious things with the somberness and rational approach they deserve – and without drama.

Under-reacting takes courage and practice. Often when the people around you are overreacting, they expect your reaction to match their own as a demonstration that you care as much as they do. Sometimes we overreact deliberately to show our concern to those of like mind, rather than express our true feelings about the situation. I have found that choosing to under-react keeps my head clear, and I am much more logical and productive than if I were to overreact.

In fact, the amazing thing is that by under-reacting, I have a more appropriate response to all that happens around me. I also know that when I under-react, people are more likely to trust me with the big and serious issues. As a leader you need and want your team and the other people around you to trust you with the big stuff – to rely upon you to make the big decisions and take strong action. When you freak out, they will think you can't handle it and go elsewhere for support or decision making.

I propose a three-step approach to learning how to under-react. First, say aloud or to yourself, "I choose to under-react." When actually spoken aloud, it signals to everyone around you that the situation or issue is serious enough that you want to be at your best to resolve it, to make the best decision, and not to be driven by emotion.

Next, physically withdraw from the issue. This is a significant step because it puts distance between you and the issue that will help you see the big picture and remain objective. I recommend that you actually simply move your feet and physically take a step back. This is a symbolic gesture, but it has tremendous results in helping you to keep cool and collected.

Finally, while taking a step back, take a breath and exhale. You have now successfully refrained from freaking out! This three-step approach has been used over and over again by my clients who report tremendous success in under-reacting. My clients who have had the courage to accept that they have a tendency to overreact and openly address it by declaring, "I choose to under-react," have built trust within their teams and among their stakeholders. It has made a significant difference for them, as I am confident that it will for you, too.

Another way to learn to under-react is to learn and practice the skills of optimism. Learning how to be optimistic will help you overcome freaking out. Optimism is an essential skill of being a better leader that will be covered later in this book. It should be noted that all of these skills must become genuine in us. Hence, next we will discuss the importance of being sincere.

S: Sincerity – Being sincere and having the highest integrity is a key component of trust.

The trait of sincerity encompasses several skills that, once learned and integrated into your character, will help you further garner trust from those around you. A good friend and expert in leadership and behavioral psychology

Dr. Ben Martinez included this story in his essay on "The 10 Principles of Leadership Power" (Martinez & Martinez, 1992):

Of all the kinds and colors of marble, the milky white Carrera is the rarest and most costly. Sculptors who lived during the Golden Age of Tuscan Sculpture claimed that it was the purest substance God ever created, and they longed for the feel of it beneath their hands. Any sculptor who was commissioned by a wealthy patron of the arts to create a statue of Carrera marble felt himself to be highly favored.

Sculpting in marble was neither fast nor easy. In addition to innate talent, it required both careful analysis and tedious backbreaking work. The artist would have to study the block of marble to determine its essential nature. He would then need to discover the direction and grain and ascertain the presence of any flaws. He had to make careful and precise plans and drawings which were in accord with the structure of the marble itself. Then, with consummate care, he would begin to chip off the superfluous marble, layer by layer, until he revealed the form he had envisioned.

Any mistake could be disastrous. If the sculptor went against the grain he could crack the marble; if he struck a blow with too much force he could mash the crystals beneath the surface, creating holes and ruining the sculpture. This seldom happened with the greatest of sculptors, who labored with infinite care and supreme sensitivity. Those with lesser talent and little patience, however, would occasionally be confronted with such a disaster. Rather than admit their blunder and lose their commission, some would resort to subterfuge.

Soft, white wax, skillfully applied, could usually disguise the damage. In outward appearance the sculpture appeared to be flawless and the defect was seldom discovered until well after the work had been accepted and the commission paid. As this practice became more common, patrons of the arts became more discerning. They refused to accept a piece of marble statuary until after a careful examination had been made to ensure that it was undamaged and contained no wax-covered flaws. The highest standard of excellence for works of white Carrera marble came to include the distinction, "sin-cere," meaning "without wax."

Eventually these two words merged to become a single word, "sincere," meaning "pure, unadulterated, whole, intact, uninjured." When the word was used to refer to works of marble the emphasis was on the fundamental wholeness of the statue and not just on the superficial or outward appearance.

The stature was expected to be good, not just look good.

Martinez goes on to say, "There is a widespread tendency today among people and organizations to resort to the same kind of tactics as the mediocre sculptor. They tend to rely too much upon outward appearances and too little upon underlying principles. They try to cover or disguise flaws and weaknesses rather than build a strong and durable foundation that will help prevent those flaws and weaknesses in themselves and others."

Being sincere is an important aspect of the TRUST formula because we don't trust people who are insincere.

We appreciate and are more willing to trust people who are sincere – who are without guile. While some people are naturally sincere, it is also a skill that can be taught and learned.

The more sincere you can become without overdoing it, the more trusted you will be. Here are a few ways to learn to be more sincere. Being truly and authentically sincere requires a certain level of vulnerability, and that can be hard for those who struggle with being vulnerable. Sincerity, to be genuine needs to come from the heart. It cannot be reduced to flattery or practiced scripted responses.

Be Humble

Later in this book I will discuss why humility is a force multiplier of leadership. For now, understand that it is also a necessary component of sincerity. Being humble is important because we are always more willing to trust a humble person than we are an arrogant person. If you want to be trusted, create organizational trust, and develop a culture of trust, learn the art of humility.

The art of being humble is not about thinking less of yourself or putting yourself down. It is about thinking of others more. In other words, humility is about giving others your genuine interest. Showing true concern for others, and not in a rehearsed way, is to be humble and sincere. When you are humble and show sincere care and empathy for someone, they have a natural desire to extend trust to you. They feel safe with you. Remember that trust is personal. Sincere humility allows people to feel that they can trust you, and so they do.

Be Grateful

Sincerity is also present when we are genuinely grateful. Something I call "Extreme Gratitude" is also covered in a subsequent chapter as a force multiplier of leadership and a key aspect to becoming a better leader. Gratitude is also a critical part of being sincere as it relates to trust. People will trust you more if they believe you are grateful and appreciative of them and their efforts. It means that you value them as an individual and not just an employee or someone you need something from.

Give Sincere Compliments

Sincere compliments are a powerful way to build trust. We naturally trust people who like us and have our best interest at heart. Giving sincere compliments is a demonstration that you care, which also helps foster trust. As with making and keeping promises, the smaller and more frequent compliments tend to be most impactful. The more frequent the compliments and expressions of appreciation, the better. Don't wait for the people around you to do something amazing in order for you to compliment them. Noticing the smaller things and commenting in a positive way does more to build trust than only complimenting them when they achieve something great. I will discuss that more in the section on the Art of Appreciation.

How you receive compliments from others can also build trust. Being gracious when you are given a compliment endears you to the giver, making it easier for them to trust you. A gracious, simple "Thank you" will usually suffice when you are paid a compliment. Another choice is to say, "You are kind. Thank you."

Be Curious

Being curious (without being nosey) is also a demonstration of sincerity. When you show sincere interest in someone or something important to someone, they see and feel that you care, which in turn builds trust. When you show interest with true intention it sends a clear message that you appreciate someone, their ideas, their opinions, and possibly their approach. Authentic curiosity is a skill that, when applied with sincerity, becomes a powerful force multiplier to help you be a better leader and will be covered in greater depth in a subsequent section.

Be Encouraging

Giving encouragement is another way to be sincere. I have met with many employees who have been designated as a "poor performer," when in reality they were discouraged and were not receiving the encouragement and support from their manager that they needed. Don't get me wrong, I am not implying that a lack of encouragement is the only reason that someone will be a poor performer. When assessing an employee's performance, it is always important to assess if it is a motivation issue or a competency issue or both.

Motivation issues can be overcome through offering encouragement and applying many of the skills and concepts covered in this book. In today's economy people are consistently being asked to do more with less and to work harder. Along with the request to do more should come sincere encouragement demonstrating that you believe in the abilities and skills of your employees and co-workers. If anyone important to you has said the words, "I believe in you," you probably know how powerful encouragement can be.

Be Genuine

You may think that being genuine goes without saying when speaking of being sincere. However, it is worth exploring because of all the managers and executives out there who are disingenuous and insincere. We all have a hard time trusting someone who is fake or manipulative. Being genuine is the opposite of being phony. It means allowing people to see you for who you are, even in your imperfection. People are more willing to trust someone who admits to mistakes, owns those mistakes, and doesn't try to cover them up, than those who are trying to fool everyone. Being genuine includes acting with the utmost integrity.

T: Transparency – There must be no hidden agendas and no strings attached.

Transparency is one of those things that can be harder to exercise than you would expect. Particularly if you are in an executive position and you know everything about the company, including confidential things that you can't share, for whatever reason. Being transparent is difficult because you can never be totally transparent – there are things you simply cannot share with anyone else.

That's just the way it is; you can not divulge all of the truth. For example, I was recently working with a company where layoffs were imminent because of restructuring. Unfortunately, a rumor got out that they were going to lay people off, and the managers were stuck. They wanted to be transparent, but they were obligated not to be. The managers did not want to lie, but they could not tell the truth. People don't trust liars. The question then is how can you develop great trust if you can't tell all the truth? You learn the art of transparency. You can be transparent and still not tell all of the truth.

No Hidden Agendas

If you don't have anything to hide or if you don't have a hidden agenda, you have nothing to fear. However, there are circumstances when you need to have a hidden agenda. So how can you not have a hidden agenda if you have a hidden agenda? I know that it sounds like a trick question and perhaps even a tongue twister. If you have a hidden agenda, you need to say you have a hidden agenda so they know that you are hiding something that you can't talk about.

Provide Context

One of the top needs of every employee is to have meaningful employment, or in other words, work that is valued and appreciated. If you have an employee who feels that he is doing stupid, meaningless, monotonous work, he will not be engaged. In turn, he will not trust his managers.

One way around that dilemma is to be transparent by providing context, meaning, and clarity about what employees do and why they do it. If you can allow your employees to see the real purpose behind their work, then they will see more meaning in their job, feel more valued, and subsequently, they'll have greater trust in leadership.

More importantly, transparency in context creates a culture of trust. When you are able to give someone context and meaning, they feel better about themselves, and they feel that you are being transparent, which allows them to trust you more. Later in this book there is a section on context as a key leadership skill.

Clarity

Clarity is about being transparent with expectations. If people don't have clear expectations, it's very difficult to hold them accountable. They will distrust you when you hold them accountable if you haven't communicated understandable and reasonable expectations. So if you give them context, "This is why you do what you do; this is how what you do affects the end results or product; and here is what I expect from you," you will go a long way to develop trust.

People want to know where they stand. They want to know their place in the organization and what is expected of them. Don't let any employee come to work wondering what you expect of them or why their job is important.

Don't Lie. Talk Straight.

As managers and executives, you may not be able to tell the whole truth on a given topic, subject, or issue. How can you tell part of the truth without lying? You do just that! Tell what you can and admit that there are things you are unable to share. It is much easier for people to trust a straight shooter, someone who talks straight. You can do that by being up front and disclaiming what you can and cannot share. The Art of Disclaimers will be covered later.

You will be appreciated for your candor and for being up front about it. Let's say as an executive that you are aware and involved in discussions about acquiring another company, and one of your employees asks you outright about a possible acquisition. This is highly confidential in any industry and in any company. You can't tell the truth and you don't want to lie. At the same time people don't like to constantly hear, "I'm sorry, I can't discuss that," which is equal to a give-away answer that acquisition discussions are underway.

I would recommend a dialog like this: "As you know, any discussions about acquisitions are highly confidential, and growth of the company is an important subject for the executive committee. There are many options for company growth that are considered all the time. Acquisition is just one strategy. If and when I can share information about any of our growth strategies, I will share them with you. Right now I need you to focus on current priorities."

Another approach would be to inquire about why your employee is so interested. It may very well be that he is more concerned about job security than he is about any company that might be acquired. If that is the case, you will build trust by addressing the underlying issue, and then you won't need to worry about answering the original question.

No Strings Attached

A very important part about building trust while engaging with people is to make sure that there are no strings attached, implied or stated. Strings are a form of mild manipulation. People want to know that they can trust you, and by having no strings attached, I mean don't be a scorekeeper. A scorekeeper is someone who remembers offenses of other people and holds it against them later. He also remembers favors he's done for you and expects you to owe him a favor at his convenience in return.

Scorekeeping is a good way to create mistrust. I am not suggesting that people should not be held accountable. I am suggesting that as a manager you don't hold things against people and use it for leverage to get your way. If you want to build trust, real sincere, long-lasting trust, do things for people with no expectation of a return. People don't like being obligated or manipulated.

Words like "always" and "never" identify a scorekeeper. A scorekeeper is also someone who keeps track of people's sick days, hours worked, mistakes, and wins. If you are the type of person who only does favors for those who have been nice to you or holds grudges against those who have slighted you, you may be a scorekeeper. Scorekeepers are trying to win – but keeping score in the office or in your personal relationships increases your chances of losing.

Don't Punish Others for Telling the Truth

Trust means that people feel they can tell the truth without negative repercussions. Being transparent also means that you allow others to be transparent, or in other words, able to trust you with the truth. People will mistrust you if you misuse the truth. A great leader learns how to emotionally handle the truth, as well as appropriately figure out what to do about it.

There are many ways to react after receiving new information, and it is a sign of wisdom to learn appropriate responses. Sometimes the best thing to do is to disregard it, while at other times finding out the truth requires immediate action. It depends on the situation. Regardless, the point here is to never punish people for telling the truth; in fact, if you want to build trust, celebrate truth-telling. This doesn't mean that you make a public spectacle of it, but appreciate it when it happens and express gratitude for the person who had the courage to tell the truth.

The T.R.U.S.T. Formula

Trust is the Sine Qua Non of being a better leader. If you don't have trust, all of the skills and techniques of being a good manager or leader will be minimized or ineffective. I have spent a lot of time on the subject of trust because it is the foundation of everything else that follows. Remember, trust is not just something you have or you don't have. It is something that can be learned, taught, acquired, built, and maintained!

If you are experiencing trouble in your organization; if your team is not living up to your expectations; if things seem harder than they should be, chances are there is a trust issue. You can't go wrong by addressing trust by using the TRUST formula. Even if you don't have a trust issue per se, it won't hurt to increase the level of trust in your organization. It can only help.

Remember that trust is personal both for the giver and the receiver. It is tied to how you feel about and perceive yourself. Trust is the one key factor to make effective all of the other skills presented in this book. Trust can be taught, learned, practiced, and developed.

The Trust Advantage In Review

☐ Trust is the Sine Qua Non of leadership. Meaning that, without it, everything else you try or do will be minimized or ineffective. Without trust, leading and managing will require a brute force effort, and your team and employees will work out of duty and likely do it with resentment. Trust gives you an advantage personally, professionally, organizationally, and financially. Remember the T.R.U.S.T. formula to build and maintain a high degree of trust.

☐ Trust is personal. Trust is a personal gift that people will give you as you build and maintain trust by applying the T.R.U.S.T. formula.

☐ Trust is not something that just happens. It can be and should be taught, built, and learned.

The T.R.U.S.T. Formula In Review

T: **Trustworthy – Take steps and actions to become more worthy of someone's trust.**

• Learn about and improve your self-worth. People who have high-self worth – those who feel good about themselves and have a positive perception of themselves – are easier to trust and to be trusted.

• Demonstrate loyalty. By demonstrating loyalty, that you have someone's back, you generate feelings of trust – you become trustworthy.

• Be predictable. People want to count on you – count on you to act, react, talk, and perform in a predictable fashion and consistent with what they consider good character.

R: Responsibility - Being responsible and accountable are a key aspect of trust.

- Be Responsible. Make and keep promises. The smaller, more frequent the promises the better.

- Be accountable. Own your actions, your behavior, and the outcome, whether you have kept your promises or not.

- Be competent. To build and maintain trust, it is imperative that you are competent; in other words, that you are able to do the job you have been hired to do.

U: Under-React – Learning not to freak out or overreact builds trust.

- Under-react rather than freak out.

- Under-react rather than be offended or have your feelings hurt.

- Under-react in a crisis or other urgent situation.

- Under-reacting helps you be at your best and problem-solve better.

S: Sincerity - Being sincere and having the highest integrity wins the trust of others.

- Be humble. If you want to be trusted, create organizational trust, and develop a culture of trust, learn the art of humility. See the later section on Confident Humility.

- Be grateful. People will trust you more if they believe you are grateful for them and appreciative of their efforts.

- Give sincere compliments. Giving sincere compliments is a demonstration that you care, which also helps foster trust. As with making and keeping promises, the smaller and more frequent compliments tend to be most impactful.

- Be curious. When you show sincere interest in someone or something important to someone, they see and feel that you care, which in turn builds trust.

- Be encouraging. Giving encouragement is another way to be sincere. If anyone important to you has said the words, "I believe in you," you probably know how powerful encouragement can be.

- Be genuine. We all have a hard time trusting someone who is fake or manipulative. Being genuine is the opposite of being phony. It means allowing people to see you for who you are, even in your imperfection.

T: Transparency - Don't have strings attached or manipulate others.

- Refrain from having hidden agendas and scorekeeping. You might be a scorekeeper if you frequently use the words "always" and "never."

- Provide clarity. Clarity is about being transparent about expectations. If people don't have clear expectations, it's very difficult to hold them accountable.

- Give context. Transparency in context creates a culture of trust. When you are able to give someone context and meaning, they feel better about themselves, and they feel that you are being transparent, which allows them to trust you more.

- Don't lie – talk straight. People don't trust liars. If you can't tell the truth, disclaim it and say what you can.

- Don't punish others for telling the truth. Being transparent also means that you allow others to be transparent, or in other words, able to trust you with the truth. People will mistrust you if you mis-use the truth.

Chapter 2:

The Optimist's Advantage

This book is about becoming a better leader – NOW! That means immediately! This book is written in such a way that the skills, concepts, and approaches herein can be implemented as soon as you put the book down. Building trust is fundamental. It sets the foundation for developing a culture of optimism.

Most of the leadership and management books published over the past 25 to 30 years have overlooked optimism as key factor of great leadership. Positive leadership is a powerful competitive differentiator, regardless of your industry or discipline. Optimism is more than just being positive; and it is more than putting on a happy face. The fact is that we would all rather work for and be surrounded by positive, hopeful people who make the best out of things, even when things don't seem to turn out for the best.

During my 32-year career with a Fortune 100 company and also coaching hundreds of executives and managers, I have witnessed the power of optimism as an impactful leadership trait. At the same time, I have seen first-hand how pessimistic leadership is just as powerful to destroy and demoralize a team.

Don't think that optimism is just looking at the world through rose-colored glasses or looking at life with a "half-full" mentality. It is much more than that and has significant benefits. As a leader, you will instill more loyalty through optimism than you will with a negative attitude or pessimism. Your employees will respond with more creativity, innovate more, and they will work harder and take fewer sick days.

You will also reap the personal benefits of optimism, as well. Those benefits include being healthier, having fewer colds and illnesses, responding to medical treatments better. You will be a better problem-solver, more creative, a better negotiator, and you will close more deals. Optimists handle change better, report lower stress levels, and get more done in less time.

MetLife, which was hiring thousands of agents a year at one point, hired Dr. Martin Seligman, a psychologist who studied optimism and positive psychology. Dr. Seligman created an optimism assessment for MetLife new-hires (approximately 15,000 agents) and followed their progress and success over a several years.

The results showed that the agents assessed as having an optimistic outlook drastically outsold their pessimistic peers by as much as 21% the first year and 57% the second year. Even more dramatic is that the top 10% of the optimists – those with the highest optimism assessment scores – sold 88% more insurance than those ranked in the highest 10% of pessimism (Optimism = Sales Success: Metropolitan Life Case Study).

Imagine the impact that even a slight improvement in optimism will make in your own organization. If you want to be a better leader and help people achieve their potential, it is essential that you become more optimistic and help others to do the same. Optimistic leaders help employees experience more happiness at work. When employees are happy, amazing things happen with tangible results. In the books *Happiness at Work* by Jessica Pryce-Jones and *The Happiness Advantage* by Shawn Achor, both authors report that happy employees (Pryce-Jones, 2010) (Achor, 2010):

- Are 47% more productive
- Are 108% more engaged
- Take 10 times fewer sick leave
- Are 50% more motivated
- Achieved their potential 40% more
- Have 28% more respect from colleagues
- Have 30% more respect from bosses
- Are 25% more effective
- Have a higher degree of innovation
- Experience more truth, less lying, and less conflict

Optimism is not something a person is just born with. While it may have something to do with a person's natural disposition and proclivity to see things positively, optimism can be learned and also taught to those around you. In my book *The Optimist's Advantage,* I share several skills that can be learned and applied immediately to reap the benefits of optimism. They include:

- The power of gratitude
- Positive storytelling
- Increasing your positive-experience set-point
- Under-react

- The power of silence
- Avoiding social comparisons
- Redefining failure to be a success
- Learning to dream big and think small
- Abundance mentality
- Emotional generosity
- Managing the path of least resistance
- How to stop throwing people under the bus
- Recharging and re-energizing
- Getting rid of negative baggage
- Finding meaning in your life experiences
- Retell the stories you tell yourself

My desire to keep this book short and to the point prevents me from elaborating on all of these skills or repeating content from my other book, so let me share a few here that I believe will make the most difference and help you become a better leader.

Discretionary Effort

Being a leader is not about title or position; it should really be measured by the willingness of people to follow you. By "follow," I mean adopting your ideals, your motives, your strategies, and directions. Being a leader is about influencing change through others. I call this discretionary effort. Discretionary effort is above and beyond what is expected and required for the job. I define leadership as inspiring people to eagerly follow you and willingly donate their discretionary effort.

Each employee owns their discretionary effort and will either donate it willingly or begrudgingly. As you become a more optimistic leader, you will increase the chances that your employees will willingly donate this discretionary effort. I was recently waiting for a flight at the Boston Logan airport. It was breakfast time, and my wife and I waited in line at McDonald's for a few Egg McMuffins.

It was amusing that as each order was called out to be picked up, the worker told each person the same exact words in the same robotic tone: "Thanks for choosing McDonalds; have a nice flight." His voice was monotone, and everyone could tell that he was saying it merely because he was told to. I could imagine that he was recently in training and the instructor told him to say those exact words to each customer.

This was not discretionary effort; this was an employee repeating what was scripted for him. Discretionary effort would have been a sincere greeting that had emotion and inflection, as well as eye contact and perhaps a bit of variety in his words. When someone goes above and beyond, not just in work activity but in attitude, as well – that is discretionary effort.

The people who work for you will be much more willing to donate their discretionary effort when they know you are grateful for what they do. Now, I have discussed this with many managers and executives who resist the idea that an employee should be thanked for doing the job they were hired to do. With that attitude, people do just that, they do what they were hired to do. But what you really want is for people to do more, to add more value than what they were hired to do. You want to inspire them to willingly and gladly donate extra effort at their discretion.

Extreme Gratitude

As a leader you need your employees to be creative, innovative, and to solve their own problems. You want and need them to invest their heart, have their head in the game, and then act with their hands and resources. One way to help your employees go beyond just "doing their job" is to be grateful.

Let me tell you of an experience that helped me see gratitude in a new light. I travel quite a bit for business and make it a habit to get to the airport early. I have a tendency to sweat when I am running late, and I would rather not go through security or get on a plane sweaty. Having traveled enough, I know that if I leave my house two hours before my flight time, I will have plenty of time for a calm airport experience.

Not that long ago I ended up running late and left my house at 6:30 a.m. for an 8:00 a.m. flight. Even before I left my house I was anxious about being late and could feel myself starting to sweat. Once in the car and on the freeway, I drove like a madman trying to make up some of the lost time. It was frustrating to see how many people were already on the freeway making my drive that much more stressful. I couldn't help thinking, "Where are all these people going? Don't they know that I need to get to the airport? How dare they get in my way." I admit that my thinking wasn't rational; but, hey, I was late and sweaty – not in the best mood.

However, an amazing thing happened that morning on the way to the airport. I took a deep breath and looked around me at all the people going somewhere at this particular time. A bit more seriously, I asked myself, "Where *are* all these people going?" The answer, when I thought about it, was quite simple – they were going to work. That thought led me to think about how different my life would be not only on that specific day but also every day if people just didn't show up at work!

It didn't take long for me to figure out that my life would be totally different, and I began to feel gratitude for the people on that freeway going to work. Instead of feeling frustrated, I felt thankful. This was definitely some sort of epiphany as I considered the impact I would experience if people just stopped going to work. When I got to the airport I was so excited to tell the TSA agent how happy I was that he showed up for work. He looked at me a bit funny, but not as funny as the gate agent, who thought I was nuts!

As a leader, think of how different your life would be today, or think of the last day you were at work and how it would be if people, your employees, didn't show up for work. It would probably be a disaster. If you have people who report to you, I am sure you have had times when someone called in sick or did not show up due to some emergency. When that happened, you scrambled either to call in favors or assign someone else to do what needed to get done.

You should be grateful that the people who work for you simply show up! Sometimes we forget that our employees have a choice, a choice to show up or not. If you adopt the attitude of being genuinely grateful that your employees show up, you will be surprised how much more work they will do.

Imagine in your own life how much a difference this attitude of extreme gratitude could make. What would it be like if, when you showed up at home after work, your spouse or children greeted you with, "I am so glad you are here! Thank you for being here!" I know it sounds a bit cheesy, but it would make you feel great; and, when done sincerely, it will make you want to do more to continue to create that positive feeling.

Imagine doing that for your employees, really making them feel that you are glad they are there and that they make a difference (even if the difference is merely that you don't have to get someone else to do their work), and they will give you their discretionary effort. They will be more loyal and they will become better employees.

The power of gratitude is that when you show gratitude for your employees – and I am not talking in terms of giving bonuses or monetary gifts – they will give you their hearts, heads, and hands in return.

Don't Throw People Under the Bus

Another aspect of optimism that you can implement immediately with dramatic results is to refuse to throw people under the bus. In the first section of this book I spent a lot of time on the TRUST formula. Throwing people under the bus creates mistrust and fosters negativity. You can easily prevent this by publically or vocally giving people the benefit of the doubt.

This does not mean that you withhold corrective action or the opportunity to guide, teach, and influence the behavior of the people around you, which should most often be done in private. What it does mean is that you simply suspend judgment until you have the facts, and when you do have the facts, address it privately.

By making this simple change you will be surprised at the loyalty and positivity this will foster. Here is an example. Let's say that you are in a staff meeting and one of your employees is complaining about someone on another team. It could be that they are depending on this person to help your employee meet a deadline or to complete a project. The temptation would be to throw the delinquent employee under the bus. By publically giving them the benefit of the doubt while encouraging your employee to work things out and pledging your support, you focus on a positive outcome without lowering yourself to belittling the employee of another team.

If the issue is serious, take your employee aside in private, get more facts, provide guidance and influence, and help them solve the problem. This sends a strong signal to your team that, in a similar circumstance, you will not be throwing them under the bus. You will have their back. This optimistic approach promotes trust.

Another way to avoid throwing someone under the bus is to refuse to judge someone based on their worst day. When you do this, and when your team sees you do this, it sends a strong message that they can take risks. They will feel that they have the latitude to be more themselves, knowing that if they have a bad day or an off day, you will not judge them based on that one day. You see, this isn't really about not throwing someone under the bus as much as it is demonstrating that you will not throw your own team under the bus and that you have their backs. When an employee knows you have their back, they will do almost anything for you.

Everything Happens for a Reason

Another facet of optimism that will help you become a better leader is the ability to accept that the phrase,

"Everything happens for a reason," is true, although incomplete. As the saying goes, if I had a dollar for every time someone has said to me, "Everything happens for a reason," I would be a wealthy man. When I was suffering with cancer for the second time, I had a serious infection that landed me in the hospital for nearly 30 days. I was miserable and thought I was going to die – that I would die from cancer, the chemotherapy, or from boredom!

It seemed like every visitor was perplexed by my situation and would attempt to console me by saying, "Everything happens for a reason." I got so sick of that phrase that I was seriously tempted to stop accepting visitors. One long, lonely day in the hospital I asked myself, "What if it's true? What if everything does happen for a reason?" The answer to my pondering came in the realization and acceptance that this phrase is indeed true, while at the same time it is incomplete. I completed the phrase in this way: "Everything happens for a reason, *but I get to choose the reason.*"

As I lay there in that hospital, I contemplated what reason I could choose for what was happening to me. Finally, I chose a reason that was personal, significant, and meaningful to me. I decided that *the reason* was that I needed to go through this experience so I could share it with others and help them. In that moment, my personal adversity changed from a curse to a blessing. In my suffering I found meaning and motivation. I had a reason to live, so that I could help people. With this new attitude I found that my pain was more manageable. I was more pleasant to visitors. And I had a brighter outlook on life even though my prognosis had not changed.

There are many things that you will face as a leader that have no immediate or logical explanation. It could be a lost sale, the loss of a contract, a key employee resigning, or legal action against you or your company. It could be a downturn in the economy or new competition in the market. All of these things, and more, can happen, and you may be at a loss for a definite explanation. And someone is bound to say to you, "Well…everything happens for a reason." Instead of taking offence, or even simply ignoring the phrase, have the courage to complete the phrase by accepting that it is true and yet incomplete. Then, you choose a reason that is personal, meaningful, and significant to you.

Don't worry about whether or not it is the wrong reason. If it is, you will know, and you will adjust things accordingly. When you choose the reason for why difficult things are happening, you will be able to think more clearly, creatively, and positively. The reason could be something as simple as needing to try harder or to learn a powerful specific lesson. It could also be something more profound and complex from a business perspective, such as learning not to take your competition for granted, or to pay more attention to the details, or to negotiate a better deal next time.

I have assisted countless clients through problems and adversity by helping them choose a personal, meaningful, and significant reason for a dilemma or problem as a way of enabling them to find a better solution. It really works, and it works in miraculous ways. However, it only works to the degree that you have the courage to find a reason that has personal meaning.

Learn to Recharge and Re-energize

Optimism, as a skill, has a lot to do with your energy and stress threshold. From an energy perspective, we all have the tendency to retreat to default behavior when we are tired, worn out, or anxious. I have met so many people who work hard, too hard, without taking the time to recharge and re-energize. Are you one of those people?

As a leader you need to be at your best, and you want your team to be at their best and bring their 'A' game. Learning what energizes you is an important part of becoming more optimistic. Not only do you need to know how *you* recharge and re-energize, it will also be important to know the answer to that for each member of your team. For example, you may have someone on your team who recharges by being alone or taking time to process. If you are constantly pestering them for an answer or micromanaging them without giving them time to be alone or to process, they will not be at their best and will feel drained and exhausted.

This concept may seem familiar to those of you who have read Stephen R. Covey's book *The 7 Habits of Highly Effective People*. The concept of recharging and re-energizing is Habit 7 – Sharpen the Saw or The Principles of Balanced Renewal. Covey says that this habit, Habit 7, surrounds the other six habits in the 7-Habit Paradigm because it is the habit that makes all of the others possible (Covey S. R., 1989, 2004).

Covey is right, and yet so many of you are ignoring this to the point that it affects your health, relationships, emotional, and spiritual wellbeing and your career. Work/life balance is a significant issue in the workplace. And when you tell your team to practice healthy self-care, and yet you don't do it yourself, you become a hypocrite.

Recently, I was facilitating an executive retreat of a small company whose revenue totaled around $25 million a year and had 325 employees. When I interviewed the executives preparing for the retreat, 90% of them said that they worked extra hours each day and spent at least six hours on the weekend working. I asked whether or not it was required or expected. Most answered that it was by personal preference and not required. In other words, they were afraid of getting behind and looking bad to their employees who had to work hard, as well.

I have found that many people are tied to email and their phones out of habit and preference, rather than because it is required. One way to consider excessive email and phone use is that it is a positive distraction that keeps managers, leaders, and employees from addressing the real issues. In other words, it provides the illusion that real work is getting done and they are staying busy, rather than implementing powerful skills and effective tools that will help people recharge and re-energize so that they can give 100% or more. Don't be tempted to confuse activity with accomplishment. That is as true for your employees as it is for you.

You recharge and re-energize by finding out what activities brings you pleasure, joy, and perhaps peace and calm. Once you've figured that out, you must schedule in the time to do those things. I enjoy alone time, and I enjoy a good fiction novel, and yet I have very little time to indulge. However, I do spend a lot of time on airplanes and have chosen not to work on the plane, to reclaim that time as my own, and use it to recharge with a good book.

I also recharge through vigorous exercise. For many years, exercise was one of those things that continually fell off my schedule to make way for more important things. Now, it goes on my calendar and does not come off! I have adjusted my sleep schedule and the time I start work to accommodate it because it is that important to me. You can do the same. If it is important enough, you will make time for it. I have found that people generally find time to do what they really want to do. Discover what re-energizes you and then develop the desire to do it and follow through. The results will be tremendous.

Recharging and re-energizing produce positive emotions, build stamina, and create the ability to handle negative emotions and experiences, thus, increasing your optimism.

Don't Let Just One Thing Ruin Your Day

Being an optimist means increasing your tolerance for things that go wrong and not letting a small thing ruin your day. Several years ago, I had come into the office to find my Administrative Assistant sobbing uncontrollably. As you can imagine, I was immediately concerned, thinking that there was a death in the family or some other sad news. Rather than going to my desk, I stopped to ask her what was wrong and how I could help. Between her sobs and blowing her nose, I learned that on the way to work she had been pulled over by the police and given a speeding ticket. She was devastated, uncontrollably so. So much so that she ended up taking the rest of the day off.

Though I was tempted to make light of the situation by saying, "Well, it happens to everyone," I resisted and chose not to minimize what she was feeling. However, I did

believe that she was overreacting and letting one experience ruin her whole day. Many of the people I meet believe
that a good day is when nothing goes wrong. That idea
itself is wrong.

Becoming an optimist requires you to set aside or minimize the bad or wrong things that happen and try not to
connect the dots between them. You can still have a great
day and stay positive even when one or a few things go
wrong. For example, not that long ago I broke one of my
teeth. The break left my tooth jagged and sharp, cutting my
tongue and causing it to bleed. It was very uncomfortable.

I quickly called the dentist for an appointment to have
my tooth repaired. Unfortunately, the dentist could not see
me that same day. I had to wait until the next afternoon.
The following day when I went to the dentist, the recep-
tionist asked how I was doing. I replied by saying, "I'm
great. Thanks." She said, "How can you be great with a broken tooth?"

My reply was, "I am great. I just have a broken tooth
– that's not going to ruin my whole day." Though she was
surprised by my answer, I was not. Small things, and even
somewhat painful things, don't ruin my day and shouldn't
ruin your day. Don't let one mere event or thing ruin your
day, and you will maintain a higher degree of optimism,
which will result in more things will going right than
wrong.

I hope you can feel my passion for the topic of optimism. Again, I have only shared a few of the many skills
that can create positivity and combat negative emotions.
It is a powerful leadership trait that can be adopted and
learned that has immediate results. If you are serious about

becoming a better leader through optimism, read my book *The Optimist's Advantage*. Become an optimist!

The Optimist's Advantage in Review

Optimism is a key differentiator in business and leadership. As you learn optimism and master it, you will become a better leader. Optimism has many benefits. One of the most profound benefits is that your employees and those around you will be more willing to donate their discretionary effort. Your optimism will have the added byproduct of creating more optimism in the people around you. You can practice the skill of optimism and reap the benefits of the optimist's advantage by applying the following principles:

- Extreme gratitude – at a minimum, be grateful that people just show up. This will change your attitude toward them, and they will respond more positively to you.

- Everything happens for a reason – but you get to choose the reason. When you chose a reason that is personal, significant, and meaningful to you, the crisis, adversity, or challenge becomes more positive and surmountable.

- Don't throw people under the bus. This sends a message that you won't throw your own team under the bus if given the opportunity. Refusing to blame and shame others not only increases positivity but also increases trust.

- Recharge and re-energize. Too many leaders and managers suffer from work/life imbalance. Learn how you best recharge and re-energize and schedule it into your calendar. Your stamina and tolerance for stress and frustration will increase, and you will influence others similarly.

- Don't let just one thing ruin your day. We all have things happen to us that can ruin our day if we allow it. Don't allow it. When something goes wrong, let it be one thing wrong instead of the demise of the whole day.

Chapter 3:

It's All About the "Who"

Great leaders know something that good leaders or mediocre leaders often forget. Great leaders know that it is all about the "who." Nothing gets done, no problems get solved, no issue can be resolved, and no success will happen without people. There is a lot of lip service on the topic of human capital. Employees are the most important asset of a company, but it is rare to see employers, directors, and managers actually treat them as such.

Becoming a better leader and inspiring people to eagerly follow you and willingly donate their discretionary effort requires you to accept and recognize that leadership is not about you! It's about everyone else. This is harder than it sounds because as a leader you are bombarded with issues and problems – sometimes more than you can manage. It is easy to get caught up in what happened, who did what, and the numbers and reports.

I have met with many managers who have adopted a Management by Spreadsheet (MBS) approach to leadership. What many spreadsheet managers miss is that no matter what the numbers say – and I don't mean to minimize the need for reporting or the reliance upon good data – it comes down to either the people who created the report, supplied the data for the report, or will implement the actions from the report or spreadsheet. No matter the 'what,' it always comes down to the 'who,' and the sooner and more seriously you accept and acknowledge this, the better leader you will become.

I recently visited a print service provider. This is a company that prints and mails much of the junk mail in the United States. I was working with the manager who managed a team of people who operated the inserting machines. During our session this manager was concerned about operational efficiencies and how, on one production line, the number of inserts had dropped below average. To this manager, it was all about the report and how to get the numbers back above average so that his boss would not be upset.

My first question was not about the numbers, not about the report, but about the people who have the first-hand knowledge of what was happening on the shop floor. At first he dismissed my question, stating that the report was automatically generated by the shop floor system. At my insistence, he put the report down and together we went to the shop floor to interact with his employees. It didn't take long to figure out that the issue was not about inserts or numbers down, but about a new employee who had not been trained effectively. The training was scheduled and problem resolved.

It is always about the 'who,' not the 'what.' In this case, we found the problem together sooner than if there had been several meetings on the topic and action plans created to further investigate, assess, and resolve the situation.

Think about the people and get them involved, and problems will be resolved quicker and, often, more efficiently.

This concept – that it's all about the 'who' – is true in every industry that I have been associated with. Becoming a better leader is about leading the people, and through the people, leading the business to create profit and revenue. Think about a sales manager who is sent daily reports on sales numbers. It would be easy for that manager to focus entirely on the numbers and forget that there were people talking to customers, taking orders, and solving customer concerns. If those same people feel inspired to follow you as a leader, you won't have to worry so much about the numbers.

Again, don't get me wrong, the numbers are important. But in this case, as in most cases, the sales were performed by the people, not the spreadsheet! The 'who' is not about placing blame or finding a scapegoat. Remember that throwing people under the bus creates negativity and will not win you trust, loyalty, or positive results. It is about truly understanding the value of human capital and respecting those humans, who want success as much as you do. Invest in them and their success, and they will invest in you and your success.

Many years ago, I attended the Program on Negotiations at Harvard Law School. Together with the Program on Negotiation was a course on Dealing with Difficult Conversations. This course was based on and taught by the authors of the book *Difficult Conversations: How to Discuss What Matters Most* by Stone, Patton, and Heen. In the class we dissected difficult conversations in order to understand the elements and the solution.

From this course I learned and adapted a valuable concept that I have been using for more than 20 years, not just in difficult conversations, but in every encounter with another human being. And it has made all the difference. The concept is this: in every encounter with another person, there are always three components or factors. These three factors are facts, feelings, and needs (Stone, Patton, & Heen, 1999).

Think about the last conversation you had. If you step back and replay the conversation, you will begin to see that, indeed, the encounter comprised facts, feelings, and needs. While all three are important, it is more important to understand and hear what people are thinking and feeling than it is to understand what the facts are. Patton, Stone, and Heen make this point: "We need to understand what the people involved are thinking and feeling but not saying to each other...this is usually where the real action is" (Stone, Patton, & Heen, 1999).

Facts

Some of you may remember the TV series "Dragnet" that aired in the late 1960s. In this police drama, which has since become a classic, the main character, Sargent Joe Friday, has a key line that he says often: "Just the facts, ma'am." The facts are the easy part. They are the 'what' of the conversation: who did what, what was needed to happen, the data in the report or analysis, and so on. It is easy, too easy, to get wrapped up in the facts.

This is where most managers and executives are comfortable. And that comfort creates a dependency on numbers, facts, reports, and analysis. So often we get wrapped up in the facts because we end up defending what we know, what we think we know, or what we believe is correct. When you have to defend yourself based on facts, it almost always ends up to be a "he said/she said" type of argument. The conversations are more about what you know and who is right and who is wrong.

In order for a resolution to occur – and by resolution I mean something other than giving in or giving up – the solution will not be found in the facts. Even if the facts are 100% accurate, the resolution will not be found by analyzing the facts. Again, I need to emphasize that facts are important, but not as important as you think. And the facts can always be addressed in a more constructive way when we move from a mindset of knowing to a mindset of learning.

Self-awareness is critical. The better you get at recognizing when you are starting to focus on the facts and are getting bogged down in them, the better you will be able to rise above the facts to get to the real issues at hand – feelings and needs. When that happens, facts will become clearer, more accessible, and have more meaning, which will make it easier for solutions to be found.

Earlier I said that facts are the easy part, and I stand by that. However, the dark side of sticking to the facts lies in the deep-seated need to be right. The need to be right is a prevalent and often toxic theme in today's social and business culture that has been ingrained in us through our upbringing, school, television shows, movies, and social media. What I am referring to is the difficulty of admitting when we are wrong, which causes us to defend ourselves with facts from a position of "knowing," rather than stepping back and considering that the other person may also be right or that what is actually right has not yet been discovered. We would make better use of facts if we would move from a position of "knowing" to a position of "learning."

All too often our assumption that we are right prevents us from learning. Kathryn Schulz, the author of *Being Wrong: Adventures in the Margin of Error,* said in her TED talk that stepping out of the bubble of always having to be right is one of the most profound things we can do on a personal and professional basis (Schulz, 2011).

Moving to a learning position allows you to move out of the story of the facts and into the real story, the story of what is behind the facts. By focusing on the facts you will be missing some key information that can help shed light on the facts or help find a faster and more sustainable solution. That information is found in the gap between what is being said and what is being thought or felt. Rarely do people say what they are really thinking or feeling. Another hidden aspect are the intentions of the other person – intentions are invisible. And though they are invisible, they can be discovered and leveraged.

Feelings and Needs

By introducing this idea of uncovering and discussing feelings and needs, many of you are already thinking that perhaps this book isn't for you. Feelings and needs sound soft, squishy, and perhaps even new-age. While feelings and needs do encompass relationship issues such as validation, recognition, and emotions, I am also talking about someone's need to be right, their feelings about the facts, as well as how they feel about you. This includes whether or not they trust you (covered in a previous section) or resent you.

Feelings and needs also include how someone is feeling physically, emotionally, and how invested they are in the subject, the outcome, or the process itself. So I can understand that at first blush, feelings and needs seem hard to deal with and interpret; but I am not asking you to be a psychologist or a behavioral analyst. By learning to draw the initial focus away from the facts and zero in on the feelings and the needs of the people and situation, you will gain both insight and extra time to learn what the real issues are and why the facts are so important to this person or in this situation.

It can also help you under-react, or in other words, keep you from freaking out. By learning to delve into feelings and needs you are able to demonstrate better leadership skills than by being drawn into arguing, defending, or supporting the facts alone. Let me share how this can be done.

Step 1. Refuse to talk about the facts without more information on feelings and needs.

Here is a real-life example of Step 1 – Refuse to talk about the facts without more information on feelings and needs. Jack and Jill were assigned to create a business case for a new product for their company. They worked closely for more than nine months to create and substantiate the business case and associated plan. The outcome of the business case and potential investment from management depended on the final presentation.

Jack felt the presentation went very well, but he could tell that Jill didn't because she left the meeting upset and possibly angry. After setting his things down in his office, Jack went to Jill's office to see why she was so mad. Jill was visibly upset and didn't want to talk to Jack and even asked him to leave her office. Jack was perplexed because he was on a high from how well the meeting with management had gone. Jack said to Jill, "I can see you are upset. At least tell me why you are upset before I leave."

With some coaxing, Jill said, "I can't believe you called me stupid in front of management!"

Jack was surprised and defended himself because he knew he had not said the word "stupid." He said, "Jill, that's absurd. The word 'stupid' never crossed my lips. That's crazy."

Jill responded, "Yes, you did. I am so mad at you. How could you do that?"

Jack said, "No, I didn't!" And it went back and forth, Jack and Jill defending their positions. Baffled, Jack finally stomped out of her office without understanding what the problem was because he was convinced that he never said the word "stupid."

While this example is somewhat simple, it illustrates the point I am trying to make. Wrapping yourself around the facts is often futile. The good news is that this scenario can be remedied and changed to a more positive one where they get to the real issues and resolve their concerns. The resolution comes from Jack refusing to talk about the facts until he has more information on Jill's feelings and needs.

Refusing to talk about the facts is the essence of moving from 'knowing' to 'learning.' It requires courage to set aside your own personal need to be right. It can be difficult and counterintuitive at first to refrain from defending your position and assuming you are correct and the other is wrong. But you gain more than we expect when you become willing to consider that you may not be as right as you think.

Step 2. Explore feelings and needs by asking open-ended questions.

An alternative scenario would be one where Jack starts with Step 1 and proceeds with Step 2 – refusing to talk about the facts until he knows more about Jill's feelings and needs. This can be done in two ways. The first is to ask a simple question without admitting anything. Jack could diffuse the situation by simply asking, "Did I?" The aim of this powerful question is to get Jill to open up and share more of her perceptions. By asking this simple question, Jack has moved from assuming he knows everything to learning more. You see, it is in *her* story that Jack will discover the real issue.

Another alternative scenario for Jack to follow through steps 1 and 2 would be for Jack to ask Jill questions that require additional information or more about her perceptions and feelings. Jack could say, "Jill, I can tell you are upset. Tell me what has you so upset over this?" Or, "I can see this is really bothering you. I don't want to get into an argument, but I really do want to know what you are feeling right now. Tell me what happened." In both cases Jack has refused to assert his version of the facts. He wants to know what is behind Jill's comment in an attempt to understand her feelings as a pathway to uncover her needs.

Step 3. Listen.

This is when it is all about the 'who,' not the 'what.' When you actually listen to what someone is saying, they will tell you exactly how they feel. Granted, they may not use words like, "I need this," or "I need that." But if you can read between the lines, they will reveal to you both their feelings and their needs. This is why you don't need to be a behavior analyst to uncover what the feelings and needs are – you will be told.

In this example, Jill revealed her needs when Jack went back and asked what was bothering her and to tell him what happened. Jill told this story: "I was so hurt when you said, 'Jill had a hard time understanding this concept until I explained it several times.'" This is a real example and it happened in just this way. Jill was upset and hurt because Jack insinuated that she wasn't smart enough to understand something until it was explained to her multiple times. As a team member Jill needed Jack to validate her contribution and expertise in front of management without diminishing it the way he did.

Without asking questions and listening, Jack would have never known what the real issue was, and her need for validation would have gone unmet. Unmet needs turn into anger and resentment. And in this case, the anger and resentment from the argument jeopardized the project. In the end, management did not fund the new product; not because it wasn't a good business case, but because Jack and Jill could not work together.

If you have an employee who is demonstrating anger and resentment, you are lucky because most of the time those feelings are hidden, which means the underlying issues go unresolved until a bigger problem evolves. Unmet needs always result in some form of negative emotion. By asking the right questions, open-ended questions that are not aimed and getting more facts, their feelings and their needs will be revealed to you.

In most situations, conversations, and encounters with another person, there are likely to be unmet needs. When those emotional needs are met, resolutions to the issue at hand come so much easier and will often present themselves. Many times, when you take the time to ask and to listen, people will solve their own problems. What I have found is that for you to be a better leader, you need to put people first – and that means putting their feelings and needs first, making them important to you. Here is a universal need: people want to have a voice and be heard. When you give them a voice and listen, you fulfill a basic need. This builds trust and will help you become a better leader.

Let me share another real example. Recently, I was coaching an executive at an upscale resort in Scottsdale, Arizona. There was an issue regarding covers in the restaurant. A cover represents a meal sold. The executive was looking at a historical report showing that covers were down by almost 20%. This represented a significant downturn during their busiest season.

The downturn was discussed in various meetings with plenty of finger-pointing, defensiveness, and blame. The general manager was under pressure for the restaurant to perform; the restaurant manager was under pressure to make her numbers; and the staff and chef were being blamed for poor service and a bland menu.

For weeks they were wrapped around the facts and were not able to find a root cause or way to fix the issue. When this was brought to my attention, I felt certain that someone at the resort restaurant understood the issue and knew what the solution was. I knew that, instead of focusing on the numbers, the executives needed to talk to the people who were experiencing the problem first-hand on the ground level – the servers. If the covers were down, then they weren't getting the tips they needed, and I felt sure they knew something.

So instead of placing blame or looking for the responsible party, I suggested they stop focusing on the 'what' and focus on the 'who.' They did. They talked with the servers and zeroed in on what the servers needed – tips. They focused on how the server's felt about the tips they were receiving and what they thought the problem was. Here is what the servers shared: "When we start to serve people, they are already frustrated because they had to choose a later seating time than they would have preferred because there were no earlier open reservations available on OpenTable. com. Then when they arrived at the restaurant, they saw that there were empty tables, which angered them."

This prompted the resort team to investigate the online reservations system. They found that there was a recent change in the system online that mistakenly showed they were busier than they actually were, and people were not able to make reservations or had to accept a reservation for a later time. The resolution was found not in the facts – but in the people – the people closest to the problem.

Let me share another recent example. Just a few weeks ago I facilitated an executive retreat for a large hotel and conference center in Denver, Colorado. As part of the preparation for the retreat, I met with each member of the executive team for a session that I call "Discover your WhY!" In the meeting, I revealed to each person their strengths, gifts, and talents.

In the session with the hotel general manager, Jennifer Atkins, it was clear that Jennifer had two gifts: insight and inclusiveness. These two gifts allowed her to quickly see beyond the facts or the 'what' (insight) to the 'who' or the people (inclusiveness). While there during the retreat, I learned that Jennifer had recently created a new position at the hotel for a Director of Customer Experience. I probed to discover the reason behind the creation of this new position.

Jennifer said, "We are measured by guest experience; not just their overall experience but also their willingness to recommend our hotel to others (called a Net-Promoter Score or NPS). The facts and the numbers only tell part of the story, so I needed to have someone (notice the 'who') responsible for the guests' experience from the moment they reach our doorstep to the moment they leave. This is a people-serving-people business, and I needed someone to create an experience for guests that results in higher NPS numbers."

Jennifer got it right. The numbers are important; it is a critical score watched by the corporate executives, but she had the insight to recognize that the numbers are about people serving guests and creating a positive experience for them. Jennifer has a great gift for being insightful to see beyond the data and the facts and to see the 'who.' This is something you can learn and develop, even if it doesn't come naturally for you.

Is this happening to you? Is your leadership being compromised because you allow yourself to be consumed by the 'what,' when you should be consumed by 'who' can lend insight or resolve the problems and issues? Problems are solved by people; actions are performed by people; you can't be a leader without the people. Put the people first by learning to start with understanding their feelings and needs, and then once you know more of the story, address the facts.

However, before I leave the topic of facts, feelings, and needs, let me say a few words about intentions. Our intent and the intent of others is often construed from the facts, and we often judge the facts and their validity on the perceived intentions of the other person. Another way to untangle yourself from the facts is to refrain from making assumptions about the intentions of someone else. You can do this by using the Art of Disclaimers, which I discuss later in this book.

It is very easy to assume intent based on the impact of a situation; for example, if we are offended by something said, we often assume that the offense was deliberate and intentional. It is quite likely not that case; but you will not know unless you first separate impact from intent. I will cover learning how to separate intent from impact in the section of this book called The Art of Disclaimers.

It's All About the 'Who' In Review

Remember that no matter what business you are in or what the nature of your team is, it is all about the people. Don't fall for the temptation of thinking that your success is found in facts or numbers. It is always about the people. Problems are solved by people. Changes are made by people. Numbers and facts are important, but great leaders know that people are the key to success.

- In every encounter three things exist – facts, feelings, and needs.
    1. Refuse to talk about the facts without exploring feelings and needs.
    2. Explore feelings and needs by asking open-ended questions.
    3. Listen – really listen.
- People, not numbers and facts, are the solutions to problems.

Chapter 4:

The Art of Appreciation

An interesting measure of good leadership is the discretionary effort put forward by employees, which I have described in earlier sections. No matter what we do or what our job is, we all have discretionary effort to offer – this is the extra effort beyond what we are paid or expected to do that adds value to our job, team, or company. Discretionary effort is donated by each individual based on how they feel about their job and who they work for.

Many times it is the discretionary effort that makes the difference between a top performer and a mediocre employee. Think of people whom you would characterize as 'going above and beyond.' That definition alone describes their donation of discretionary effort – the effort above and beyond what someone is asked or compelled to do that is donated at their discretion.

When people work for someone they trust, who appreciates them, has an optimistic disposition, and is concerned about their feelings and needs, they are more willing to donate their discretionary effort without expecting much in return. One of the keys to inspiring your employees to donate their discretionary effort willingly is to truly and sincerely appreciate them. When an employee feels appreciated, especially appreciated for donating their discretionary effort, they feel good about the donation and most often are willing to donate more and go out of their way to please you.

This type of appreciation is an art form that can be mastered. It is about more than giving compliments and praise; it is about giving appreciation. In fact, I will go as far as to say that offering sincere appreciation combined with praise will do more to create positive and desired behavior than any other incentive or reward.

Unfortunately, we have all been brought up or trained as employees with a quid pro quo mindset, expecting that if we do this, we will get that. In other words, if we do what is right, expected, or more, then we will get a reward. However, any attempt to manipulate or change the behavior of others based on incentives may prove to be successful in the short run, but it is not sustainable in the long run and can even do more harm than good (Kohn, 1999). My recommendation is not that rewards and incentives go away, but recognize that they have their place as a reward and not as a motivator for long-term positive change.

There is a difference between praise and appreciation. To understand the difference between praise and appreciation, it is important to understand them as tools that accomplish different things. Praise is an excellent tool for acknowledging and recognizing someone for a job well done – with an emphasis on the doing. Appreciation, on the other hand, is a tool that recognizes someone for who they are. Discretionary effort is donated more freely when both praise and appreciation are used. To further explain and relate to the previous section, praise is about the *what* and appreciation is about the *who*.

The difference between praise and appreciation follows the distinction between self-worth, self-esteem, and self-confidence. In my book *I AM STRONG*, I explain the difference between these three important aspects of how a person feels about themselves (Wilkinson, 2011). I don't need to repeat that here, but from a leadership perspective and for the purposes of understanding the Art of Appreciation, it is important to note the distinction. Self-worth is more about who you are, whereas self-esteem and self-confidence are more about what you do. There is additional explanation of this concept in the bonus chapter at the end of this book.

For many people and in much of the current personal development literature, self-worth, self-esteem, and self-confidence are used synonymously. In contrast, I consider them as distinct and different from one another; and while they are all important, they can be addressed differently with tremendous results. At the end of the day we would all like our employees to be confident and have a high regard for themselves without being arrogant. Praise and appreciation can help them accomplish just that.

However, before I get into the mechanics of the Art of Appreciation, it is also important to understand the emotions someone suffers after a blow to their self-esteem, self-confidence, and self-worth. When we do something wrong, make a mistake, or do something stupid, we take a hit to our self-esteem and self-confidence, and this hit takes the form of feelings of incompetence. When our self-worth takes a hit, we can have some intense feelings of inadequacy.

From experiences in school, at home, and at work, we have likely been trained to think that incompetency and inadequacy are the same. They are not. Imagine this. Let's say that you have a teenager who brings home a less-than-stellar report card when you know they are smart and capable. In reality, the difference between a 'C' and an 'A' isn't necessarily intelligence, but effort. In other words, the difference is in what they did, not in who they are.

If you talk to your teenager about their grades, chances are that they will think you are calling them stupid – they will feel inadequate when they should be feeling incompetent. We have all been taught this way – to think that when we do something wrong, or we don't do enough, we are inadequate. But we are not. At most, we are incompetent, but certainly not inadequate.

Praise is meant to recognize people for what they did or do – acknowledging that they are not incompetent, but competent; that they did something well. Appreciation is then used to help your employees feel adequate – to recognize them for who they are. When combined, praising them for good effort or work and appreciating them by recognizing a particular strength or gift that helped them perform that work will inspire your employees to do more, or rather, to donate their discretionary effort to you.

You can think of it this way: if you had to choose between two uncomfortable emotions, which would you rather experience – feelings of incompetency or feelings of inadequacy? I have asked this question to thousands of people. I have found that this is a more difficult question than I anticipated. But I have found that most people, if they had to choose, would chose to feel incompetent rather than inadequate. Why? Because it is easier to overcome feelings of incompetency than it is to overcome the feeling that you can never be good enough.

You may remember that competency was discussed previously in the section on trust. You overcome feelings of incompetency by becoming competent, learning from your mistakes, and doing better. Knowing this, it is important to praise accurately for what people do and appreciate them for who they are – to help them feel more competent while helping them feel more adequate. Appreciation is not just used to make people feel good, although that does happen; it also increases output and effort because they are being recognized for who they are – something that we all desire and sometimes crave.

Knowing the difference between praise and appreciation is the foundation of the Art of Appreciation. Of the two, praise may be a bit easier from the perspective that you know what your people do or what they should be doing. You are aware of their accomplishments and their short falls. The hard part about praise is simply doing it.

Now, I have met many leaders who are afraid of praising their people. One client said to me, "If I praise my employees, they are going to expect a raise at the end of the year. I don't have the budget for raises, so I don't want to praise them and disappoint them later." At the same time, the reason I was working with him was because his team had given him very low scores on a 360-degree assessment. His team was rebelling because they felt their hard work was being ignored – and it was. Don't fall into this trap. You can praise your people without obligating yourself to hand out raises and bonuses. Later on you will learn how the Art of Disclaimers will enable you to do this quite well.

Praise can also be tricky in that it may be hard to find the right balance between not enough praise and too much. Give too little and people will resent you; too much and it becomes insincere and diminishes the positive impact it can have. I always recommend that my clients err on the side of too much, rather than too little, however. The problems created with too much praise are much easier to deal with than when there is not enough. However, this recommendation is only valid when appreciation is also used. Don't get me wrong; I would not recommend that you combine praise and appreciation every time, but the combination of the two, when used appropriately and sincerely, will increase your effectiveness as a leader and motivate your people to freely donate their discretionary effort.

Appreciating someone for who they are requires that you know who they are. I have met far too many executives and managers who don't have a clue about the people who work for them. If you are an executive, you don't need to know everything about everyone. And I am not talking about knowing personal details about every employee. What I am talking about is knowing enough about your employees that you can appreciate them for their strengths, talents, and gifts.

Let me use an example of combining praise and appreciation to demonstrate what I mean. You might say something like, "Joan, well done on landing the Acme account. I know that took a lot of time and effort. You did a great job. However, what I appreciate most about you is your work ethic and persistence. Thank you." In this example, notice the separation of what Joan did (land the account) and who she is (her work ethic and persistence). This means that even when Joan is not performing at her best, she will know that you think she has a good work ethic and is persistent, and she will rise to that acknowledgement.

However, in order for this to happen, you will need to know that she has a strong work ethic and that she is persistent. My challenge to you is to start looking at your employees differently. Start seeing them for who they are, not just what they do. Observe and remember their strengths and the value they bring to you, the team, and the company. When you do this and combine praise and appreciation together, you will be amazed at how much more your people will do and how much more loyal they will become, which is the essence of discretionary effort.

Interestingly enough, this powerful combination of praise and appreciation is also effective when you need to give critical feedback. I call this using a praise sandwich. Critical or negative feedback is always more effective when the person knows you appreciate them for who they are. When we know that someone appreciates us, we are more likely to accept negative feedback and we are more willing to learn from our mistakes.

I will tell you how it's done. Let's say that you have an employee who has missed two very important deadlines and you need them to acknowledge it and correct it for future projects. Your conversation, using a praise sandwich, could go like this: "Jack, you have worked here for almost five years and have had increasingly more responsibility over the years. Your work has been good; in fact, at times your work has been exceptional." Notice the praise – focusing on what he has done or did recently.

Now comes the negative feedback. "However, the deadlines on your last two projects were missed. This seems unlike you, and I wanted to give you the opportunity to discuss this and see what help I can offer. As you know, this is unacceptable and I want to help you get back on track." This is just a brief example, knowing that, in reality, a discussion with your employee would certainly follow. The other part of the sandwich comes into play as you conclude the discussion, and it could go like this: "Jack, before you go I want to let you know that I appreciate you. I appreciate your diligence and loyalty to this team and to the company. I know you can make the changes necessary."

The praise sandwich really works. It helps people put the negative feedback into context and gives them a foundation for improvement. Granted, these few examples are simple ones and you will need to adjust to fit the circumstances. As you become more comfortable with the art of appreciation and use it effectively with the right amount of praise, your people will respect you more. As that happens, you can employ the praise sandwich to help your people grow and improve.

You will become a better leader by understanding the difference between praise and appreciation and use them appropriately. When used in combination, they will motivate your employees to donate their discretionary effort freely – they will do more for you and do it willingly.

I can't leave this topic without saying few words about employee performance evaluations. My experience, and that of the majority of people with whom I have worked, is that performance evaluations should be one of the most motivating and rewarding meetings with your manager. And yet they are almost always the opposite. In most cases, performance evaluations demotivate employees. Reducing the motivation of employees works against the best interests of the manager and company and diminishes effectiveness, profits, and success.

I believe the reason for demotivating performance evaluations is that there are a lot of expectations and anticipation surrounding the official evaluation. In some companies, pay and promotions are directly tied to ranking, which is tied to the annual performance evaluation. The Art of Appreciation is a great tool to use in a performance evaluation, and when combined with praise in the right way, the performance evaluation can evolve to be motivating and instrumental in inspiring your employees to donate their discretionary effort. Here are a few steps to achieve a more inspiring evaluation:

1. Absolutely no negative surprises: if there are development issues or other negative feedback that is to be included in the evaluation, instead share that with your employee no later than 90 days before the evaluation. I know that this adds a bit of work to your preparation, but it will pay off. At least 90 days before the official evaluation, share constructive feedback with your employee using the praise sandwich approach. Make sure they leave this meeting aware of needed improvements but feeling your sincere appreciation for who they are, as well. With many of my clients I ask them to call this an 'accountability session.'

2. If you haven't already done so, learn what you can about your employees. Specifically, learn

who they are so that you can appreciate them effectively. You may have to do some research and you may actually have to talk to them and ask them questions about who they are. But do the homework. It will pay off.

3. Prepare the evaluation using combinations of praise – call out what they did well and actually praise them in the official document. Add appreciation and document it in the evaluation.

4. Deliver the evaluation and be very specific about the praise and appreciation. Then, and this is important, tell your employee that you don't need to discuss any of the development issues because they have already been discussed previously in the accountability session but are noted in the evaluation. DON'T rehash what you have already discussed.

Clients of mine, though they struggled with this at first, have used this approach with tremendous success. This approach is not perfect and there may be some cases when it does not apply, but it really does work.

The Art of Appreciation In Review

There is a difference between praise and appreciation. You will become a better leader as you learn the difference and then leverage it to your advantage, as well as to the advantage of your employees. Praise is important and needed, but appreciation will have a more profound and longer lasting impact. You can praise and appreciate your employees without creating an expectation of a raise or other reward.

- Praise is about what someone does – what they do.

- Appreciation is about who they are – their character, their style, their approach, their insight, gifts, talents, and strengths. In order to appreciate someone for who they are you have to get to know them.

- Negative feedback – consider using a praise sandwich where you first praise, give the constructive feedback, and then sandwich it with appreciation. Make sure your employee hears the appreciation. When they do, there is a greater chance of them making the needed changes to improve.

- Performance evaluations can be motivating by using praise and appreciation appropriately and following these steps:

  1. There should be absolutely no negative surprises. Cover any negative feedback no less than 90 days before the formal evaluation in a meeting that I often refer to as an accountability session.

  2. Do the homework to find out more about your employees in order to appreciate them more completely and effectively.

  3. Prepare the evaluation using combinations of praise and appreciation, and document it in the evaluation. The evaluation should be a positive, motivating experience!

4. Deliver the performance evaluation, and be very specific about the praise and appreciation without discussing any of the development issues because they have already been discussed previously and are noted in the evaluation. DON'T rehash what you have already discussed.

Chapter 5:

The Art of Disclaimers

We are all familiar with disclaimers. You cannot watch TV without seeing a pharmaceutical commercial that is filled with rapid-fire disclaimers, such as, "Don't use this if you are pregnant, have high blood pressure, etc." The pharmaceutical companies use disclaimers to reduce their risk of legal liability. We are all familiar with safety disclaimers on products, such as blow dryers, curling irons, fans, and other electrical products, where we are warned to not use them in the bathtub or submerge them in water.

In leadership, management, and relationships, disclaimers are not necessarily used as warnings to prevent injury or side effects, but they can be used effectively to provide clarity, insight, and understanding. The Art of Disclaimers is powerful enough to warrant an entire book on the subject; but it is so simple in application that it can adequately be covered in a short section of this book. Do not let the brevity of this section detract from the importance and power of this skill.

In any conversation or encounter with another person or group, the probability of miscommunication is relatively high. One reason for a lot of miscommunication is that we are constantly interpreting what people say by our own perception of their motive and intent. Based on my own experience and observation, we are rarely 100% correct in interpreting someone's motive and intent – even when we know the person really well.

My wife and I will soon celebrate our 37th wedding anniversary, and even though we have known each other for more than 37 years, we still have a hard time understanding each other's motive and intent sometimes. If it happens with people who know each other so well, imagine how hard it is when you don't know the other person. When it comes to motive and intent, we make huge assumptions based on our own perceptions and values.

Earlier, I recommended that you separate motive and intent from impact to help you understand the feelings and needs of others when in conversation with them. The Art of Disclaimers is used to *disclaim* your motive and intent so that the person with whom you are communicating does not have to guess or assume. Stating up front what your intentions are and what your objective is allows the listener to have a framework from which to receive what you are saying and understand you better. This allows both you and the person to whom you are communicating to separate motive and intent from impact.

Let me give you a quick example. As I have already mentioned, I travel quite a bit and often arrive at my hotel prior to the established check-in time. By using disclaimers, I have a better chance of being able to check in early. Instead of just asking for an early check-in, I make a disclaimer prior to the request. I say, "I know I'm early but I am hoping you may have a room ready." Simply adding "I know I am early" disclaims my awareness of their policy, and I am asking for an exception.

These simple words clarify my intent (hope versus demands or expectation of early check-in) and reveal that I am not being arrogant or pushy and create open conversation that, in all but a few cases, has allowed me to get a room early. There have been many times when the person attempting to check in right after me didn't get a room until later. Disclaimers really work.

Another example to help explain the use and power of disclaimers happened when I was working with a client from Bulgaria who spoke with a slight accent and with intensity. One of her concerns was that her team and other stakeholders in her organization perceived her as being angry. In fact, she had received feedback on multiple performance evaluations that she came across as angry. After just a few sessions with her it was clear to me that Debbie was not angry at all; passionate, yes – but angry, no. However, because of her accent and her strong energy, I could see how others might assume that she was angry.

I coached her to start using disclaimers to 'disclaim' her mood, intent, and motive in conversations to reduce the incorrect assumption that she was angry. She would say, "I know that my accent and passion about this subject may cause you to think that I am angry – but I am not. I just feel strongly about this."

This small and short disclaimer and other versions of it made a significant difference. People were no longer misinterpreting her mood and motive and started listening to her more. In fact, in just a few months after starting to use the Art of Disclaimers in this way, she was approached by management to accept a promotion. Note that she did not have to change her personality. She merely exposed and clarified her intent. The use of disclaimers has many applications, from disclaiming your mood, motive, and intentions, to your feelings, needs, and wants.

As I mentioned in an earlier section, in any encounter or communication the feelings and needs are more important than the facts. Learning the art of using disclaimers enables you to convey your feelings and needs in a constructive and actionable way. For example, Tom, who had worked for Andrew for a few years asked for a raise. The topic itself made Andrew feel uncomfortable and awkward because he was unable to give an off-cycle raise and didn't want to offend Tom by saying no. But his hands were tied.

He used disclaimers in this way. Andrew said, "Tom, you are a good employee and I realize how hard it must be to ask for a raise. However, this topic makes me feel uncomfortable and awkward. Uncomfortable because if I can't give you a raise, I don't want you to take it the wrong way; and awkward because I don't want the lack of a raise to impact what I believe is a good relationship between us."

Andrew went on to tell Tom why he was unable to give him a raise and also used the Art of Appreciation with Tom. Andrew was pleased to tell me that Tom took it well, and although Tom was disappointed, their relationship was even better than before. Tom appeared to be more motivated, as well.

Another way to use disclaimers is to state your needs and objectives up front so that people know what your expectations are. I have a good friend who is an exceptional problem solver. He is so good at problem solving that he will often have a hard time just listening to me, as he wants to jump in and give recommendations and advice.

Knowing this about him, I disclaim my needs and objective before I start a conversation. I might say something like this, "Bill, I know you are good at solving problems and usually have good ideas for solutions, but right now I just need you to listen and not try to solve this for me." Disclaiming my needs in this way sets the stage for a more productive conversation by preventing the frustration I feel when Bill tries to solve the issue rather than just listen.

To use disclaimers in this way, you will need to recognize and be aware of your needs and objectives. The more you can assess and know your needs, the better your disclaimers will be and the more effective your communications will be. Recently my wife and I watched five of our grandchildren while my daughter and son-in-law spent ten days in Europe. My 10-year-old granddaughter Lyssa, who isn't as quick to follow directions as I would like, is also very sensitive to my impatience, especially when I raise my voice.

Knowing this about Lyssa and also knowing that I needed her cooperation, I used disclaimers. I told her, "Lyssa, I know you don't like it and hurts your feelings when I get impatient and raise my voice. But I need you to clean up your mess on the table. I feel frustrated that you haven't done what I asked. Will you please clean it up now?" As you can see, this is also another form of under-reacting, which was discussed earlier. It is much more likely to garner cooperation than using anger or negative leverage.

As you can see, disclaimers are a powerful skill that integrates all of the other skills in this book. Using disclaimers is a bit of an art form that needs to be practiced. To use disclaimers effectively, you need to become more aware of the situation, yourself, and the people around you.

Disclaimers also have power to assist you to be a better and more effective leader, as you help others disclaim their motive, intent, and objectives to you. I use this often to help me be a better listener and communicator. For example, if someone starts to tell me something, and it is not clear to me what role they want me to play, I get them to disclaim their intent to me by simply asking them. It could go something like this, "Do you want me to just listen or do you want me to help you resolve this?"

If I am not sure what a person is feeling, I ask them to disclaim their feelings to me. I might say, "You seem angry. However, I am not 100% sure that is what you are feeling. What is it you're feeling?" By addressing feelings, we are more likely to come to mutually agreeable solutions and build trust.

I also use disclaimers in emails and when setting calendar appointments. If someone's calendar shows 'busy' and I need them to reorganize their appointments, I will often include in the invite, "Your calendar shows busy, but I am hoping that you can change things around…" This disclaims that I have done my homework and did notice that they were busy. By respectfully acknowledging this, I am more likely to get the cooperation I need.

Or if I have to re-send an email to someone because I didn't get a response, I disclaim, "I know you are busy and this probably got buried in your in-box, so I am resending this to you…" I realize that for many of you this sounds like an apology or it sounds like I am sugar-coating issues and conversations. Disclaimers are not apologies but acknowledgments; and they are not sugar-coating, but a powerful way to improve and enable better communication and trust. The side benefit is that people will feel more safe to open up to you and will see you as a better communicator.

Disclaimers do not give you permission to be rude or sarcastic. I often use a disclaimer like this in private coaching sessions: "I am going to put you on the spot," or "My goal with this next question is to make you feel some discomfort." Even so, it does not give me an excuse to be disrespectful. Disclaimers, just like anything else, can be misused and abused. If you were to disclaim that you are really angry, that doesn't give you the right to physically attack someone or to be verbally abusive.

The use of disclaimers is meant to improve and enable effective communication and to share your motive and intent in any conversation, not an excuse to be mean. Disclaimers can fit any personality and almost any circumstance. Give it a try. You may be surprised at the results. The Art of Disclaimers is one skill that you can try immediately that will help you quickly become a better leader.

The Art of Disclaimers In Review

Don't expect people to be mind-readers; in other words, to know your intentions, motives, objectives, and mood. Tell them through a disclaimer. This will help you have much more effective communication and improve all of your relationships.

- People can't read your mind – use disclaimers to communicate your motive and intent.

- Use disclaimers to convey your mood – if you are angry, frustrated, or feel awkward, disclaim it.

- Use open-ended questions to get others to disclaim their motive, intent, feelings, and needs to you.

- The use of disclaimers is not a justification to be rude or mean.

Chapter 6:

Authentic Curiosity

As a young man in my twenties I was fortunate to work beside a man, Dr. Benjamin Martinez, whom I quoted earlier in the section on trust. I consider Dr. Martinez to be one of the best leaders I have known. He taught me foundational principles of leadership that are timeless and extremely effective. From Dr. Martinez I learned many of the leadership principles that have been canonized by authors such as Stephen R. Covey, Tom Peters, Peter Drucker, and more. One of those timeless and powerful principles is what I call authentic curiosity. In Covey's book *The 7 Habits of Highly Effective People*, he refers to this principle as, "Seek first to understand and then to be understood," Habit number 5 (Covey S. R., 1989, 2004).

The people around you, your employees, peers, superiors, family, and friends all have the basic need to claim their voice and be heard. Additionally, the people who work for you and want to follow you as their leader want to know you care. Theodore Roosevelt once said, "No one cares how much you know, until they know how much you care." There are many ways to show how much you care. Some ways are easier or harder than others.

So far in this book we have talked about being sincere as part of the formula to build and maintain trust, as well as the Art of Appreciation and the skill of optimism, which will all contribute to demonstrating how much you care. Being authentically curious is another way and one of the key skills of great leaders and managers.

Authentic curiosity is a means to establish and demonstrate trust. It is also a powerful method of practicing meaningful delegation, time management, and boosting your effectiveness as a leader. Authentic curiosity also contributes to the skill of being confidently humble that will be covered later.

This type of curiosity is not about being nosey. It is not meddling or manipulative interrogation. It is the art of being truly interested in what another person has to say, what they think, and prompting them to have a voice and to solve their own problems. It is a means of truly seeking to understand a person or situation before jumping in and solving the problem.

When you are authentically curious you put yourself in the position of a trusted advisor, rather than a know-it-all or authoritarian. No one likes a know-it-all. And no matter what anyone will admit to you, there are very few people who like to be told what to do. If you find yourself in a position of having to proclaim your authority or title in order to get things done or to get people to do what you expect of them, this is an indicator that something needs to change.

An authoritative style of management isn't sustainable in the long term. Being curious, authentically curious, allows you to maintain your authority and express your opinion in a way that becomes more acceptable to the people who work for you. When people see you as a trusted advisor, you are able to elevate your contribution and be seen as a leader, rather than a boss.

To be authentically curious is a simple skill to master. First, make it a point to refrain from answering a question or addressing an issue without some level of investigation. Don't think that I am advocating that you become a skilled interrogator or that you simply stop giving your opinion. What I am suggesting is that you ask more questions – thoughtful, insightful, and open-ended questions – that draw a person out and give them permission to say what they are thinking or come up with ideas and solutions on their own.

Every day you are bombarded with decisions that need to be made and issues that need to be solved. I have worked with many executives and managers who derive a lot of value from being the 'go-to' person. While at the same time, they ask for my help to manage the mountain of email and other activities on their plate because they are just that – the 'go-to' person. Here are some sample questions that demonstrate curiosity effectively:

- "What do you think we should do?" This question encourages a person to think about the solution and demonstrates trust and humility. When done authentically, it sends a signal to the other person that you are willing to listen to them and consider the options that they bring forward.

- "What is your opinion?" When you sincerely ask someone for their opinion, you send a strong message to that person that you are willing to listen to them, consider what they have to say, and that you respect them. This is a powerful message of validation that so many employees seek. I have seen this question raise the morale of individuals and increase their donation of discretionary effort.

- "Is there any reason why you may not be able to handle this on your own?" This needs to be asked in an empowering tone that signals that you believe they are capable of handling the problem or issue. Now, you may say, "This question isn't really a question of curiosity, as much as it is a tactic to get someone to do what they should be doing in the first place. When this question is asked in supportive and teaching tone, it is a real and sincere question that communicates your belief that this person can, in fact, handle the problem on their own. It is also an opportunity to discover how they feel about their competency and address concerns if there are any.

- "I can tell this is important to you. Can you tell me why?" I use this question quite often when someone is being passionate, angry, or seems to be in a rush. By asking this question you give them the opportunity to take a breath and explain what they are feeling rather than argue facts. You will recognize this question from the section above on facts, feelings, and needs. It is a very important question that will show your interest.

- "Can you help me understand this issue better?"
  Not only does this question signal to the other person that you are interested and that you care, it also gives you the benefit of hearing their thought process and how they may perceive the problem. An ancillary benefit is that it gives you more time to assess the problem, situation, or circumstance.

Another way to demonstrate authentic curiosity is to make it a practice to avoid being the first one to talk. I don't mean to say that you stand there with your mouth closed and refuse to speak before someone else says something. What I mean is: don't just jump in with your own agenda, your own topics, or points. Let someone else kick things off. This is a small gesture that will make a significant difference. You can facilitate this by simply saying, "Before I jump into my topics or questions, I would like to hear from you first."

There are many, many more questions that demonstrate curiosity that I could outline here, but I am sure that you get the point. When you demonstrate authentic curiosity you become a better leader. Part of becoming a better leader is to enable your team, employees, and the people around you. Authentic curiosity does just that.

Showing curiosity and asking thoughtful questions empowers people to think for themselves and to solve problems and issues. It raises the contribution of the team, organization, and company. This is true in your personal relationships, as well. If you have children, try being more curious about them, their interests, concerns, dreams, beliefs, thoughts, feelings, and opinions. You may be pleasantly surprised by what you learn.

As I conclude this section on authentic curiosity, let me be clear about one thing. Just as with all of the skills and principles in this book, curiosity can be overused. When it is overused or used in manipulative or interrogative manner, it will have a negative impact. If the people around you begin to believe you are being nosey or that you ask questions because you don't know the business, the answers, or how to get things done, your curiosity becomes a liability.

I was once in an organization where the Global Sales Manager asked so many questions that everyone began to feel that he did so in order to disguise the fact that he had no opinion of his own or that he didn't want to make a decision. Don't fall into this trap. Curiosity needs to be applied in a sincere and authentic way without overusing or overdoing it. If you *only* seek to understand, you may never be understood.

Authentic Curiosity In Review

Curiosity, when authentic, is a strong message that you are interested and care. This goes a long way to win trust. Curiosity is not just about learning things. It has the side benefit of enabling your team to think for themselves. They will actually become more self-sufficient and relieve you of a lot of minutia and problems that your team can solve on their own. Curiosity also shows that you respect your employees, thereby increasing employee engagement and the donation of discretionary effort. You can show your interest by practicing the following:

- Don't speak first – let others speak first.
  - Ask good open-ended questions.

- o "What do you think we should do?"
- o "I can see this is important to you. Can you tell me why?"
- o "What is your opinion?"
- o "Is there a reason you may not be able to handle this on your own?"
- o "What do you think the best course of action would be?"

As a word of caution, don't overuse or abuse curiosity.

Chapter 7:

Context, Context, Context

For many years I worked to improve employee engagement at a Fortune 100 company. For a short time, I was even given the title of Executive Advisor on Employee Happiness. I was in the unique position to report to the general manager of a small division whose goal was to significantly improve the employee engagement scores on the annual employee survey. My approach was to first ignore the survey numbers and the comments and instead zero in on the most important relationship at any company – the relationship between an employee and their direct manager.

There are numerous studies that indicate that when the employee and immediate manager have a trusting and productive relationship, employee engagement is higher. One such study was performed by the Dale Carnegie Training organization. The report states: "Employees perceive their value as an individual through the prism of the immediate supervisor... It is said that employees don't leave companies; they leave people. What managers do, how they behave, what they say and, importantly, how they say it affects employees' attitudes about their jobs and the organization as a whole. Employees who are unhappy and dissatisfied with their immediate supervisors are less likely to identify with the organization's vision and more likely to be absent or to resign" (Training, 2012).

That led me to focus on the relationship between managers and their direct employees and seek to help managers foster and create a positive relationship with each individual. One aspect of that relationship that I focused on is the basic need of the employee to know that their job has merit and that what they do is meaningful and significant. When a worker, regardless of whether or not they work on an assembly line, in a factory, or in a cubicle, understands how their job contributes to achieving the final goal or creating the finished product, they will be motivated and do better work. Every single employee needs to know and wants to know that what they do matters.

It is demoralizing to go to work each day thinking that your job doesn't matter or not knowing how what you do fits into the big picture. Employees translate that into thinking that *they* don't matter. This is where context comes into play. We have all heard it said that one of the most important aspects of retail businesses is location, location, location. For leaders and managers, where their employees are concerned, it's all about context, context, context! One critical aspect of effective leadership is helping your employees feel that their job has significant purpose. They need to know the context of their job as it relates to the big picture of the business and how they contribute to the overall success of the company.

As a young man working my way through college, I took a job with a company that manufactured printed circuit boards. At the time I knew nothing about printed circuit boards and had no idea what they were used for. My job was to do the gold plating for the interface section of the board. I believe I was adequately trained to follow the process and visually inspect each board as it was dipped into multiple solutions so that the gold would adhere to the board. It was dull, tedious work.

After a few weeks, I desperately sought another position within the company, a position that wasn't so boring. I started to look outside the company, as well. My apparent boredom caught the attention of my supervisor, who called me to discuss the quality of gold plating that had fallen off since my first two weeks. I could tell that he was disappointed and, at the same time, he was aware that the job itself was not hard; it was the monotony. The boredom was maddening.

To his credit, he didn't chastise me for the recent poor-quality output. Instead he took me on a full tour of the facility and then showed me pictures of the devices the circuit boards would be installed in. I had never seen such devices. He explained that the circuit boards were installed in medical devices that monitored blood flow in hospital ICUs. I had no idea that the boards I worked on were used to save lives!

This supervisor gave me context and meaning. I saw the context of my small part in the whole process. Understanding the context gave me the motivation to work harder, pay more attention, and feel that my job made a difference. The job itself did not change, but my perspective did. I ended up continuing that job for many months without another quality issue. This is the power of context. If you want to be a better leader, help your people, your co-workers, and stakeholders understand the context of their jobs.

Help them to see how what they do is important and why it matters!

Recently I was working with a client who held the position of Executive Director of Housekeeping at a renowned private golf club in Scottsdale, Arizona. This club is one of the largest and most prestigious golf clubs in the country. It caters to wealthy members who expect the best. This particular director was having a hard time with quality control over the various aspects of keeping the club clean and maintained. He had experienced significant turnover and found it difficult to hire people who would stay for more than a few months.

As we talked about new employees and how they were on-boarded and trained, it was clear that this man knew his job. He knew every aspect of the club and could do any of the necessary jobs himself. He took pride in having things 'just so.' It became apparent to me that the issue was not about who he hired, and for the most part his on-boarding and training was good from a tactical perspective.

I shared with him the concept of Context, Context, Context and asked him to go back to his employees and not only train them how to clean a flagstone floor or shampoo a carpet overnight but also to help them see how each job contributed to the overall member satisfaction and profit of the club. I encouraged him to give each job meaning and context for the employees. I asked him to help them internalize that not only their work but also their attitudes and appearance made a difference to the experience of the guests at the golf club. Over a period of 90 days his turnover had reduced to almost zero and he was spending less time fighting fires and more time enabling employees to do more.

Context makes a difference. As you help your employees internalize the context and meaning of what they do, they will turn to you as their leader and will be inspired to do more than you ask them to do. When an employee understands and internalizes the context of their job and role, they donate more of their discretionary effort. As they do so, you become a better leader.

Context, Context, Context In Review

Remember that people need to feel that their jobs have meaning. You may need to do some homework on what that meaning is and then learn to communicate it so that each employee feels that what they do is important. It is likely that you need to repeat this over and over again because employees may not be able to see or feel that meaning on their own through the course of their work. You may want to consider a mission and vision statement for your company, organization, or team. Let everyone participate in the creation of those statements. Mission and vision statements help establish context and meaning.

Chapter 8:

Confident Humility

I often ask my clients to tell me about someone they despise and describe what is despicable about them. More than 90% have described someone who is arrogant. As much as people dislike arrogant leaders, they appreciate leaders who are confident, bold, brave, outspoken, and *humble*. It is a daunting list and seemingly contradictory to be bold, brave, and outspoken, while still humble. But it is actually not a paradox at all.

Being humble does not mean being weak or yielding. Humility is not thinking less of yourself but thinking of yourself less. It is demonstrating that you have a high regard and respect for the feelings and needs of others. Earlier in this book I spoke of trust as the Sine Qua Non of leadership. Without trust, all of your efforts as a leader would be diminished.

Humble leaders are trusted more than arrogant leaders. If you want to be a better leader, then learning how to be more humble is an imperative. This does not mean you need to be mild-mannered, soft-spoken, or shy to be humble. You can be humble and still be bold and confident. Following are a few things you can do to demonstrate humility while still being confident.

Give credit where credit is due.

I can't even count the times I have heard employees talk poorly and express disrespect for their manager for taking credit for what an individual or the team had done. Confident humility is being brave enough to forego taking credit when it is owed to colleagues or others on your team. The trust and respect you gain from your employees and coworkers is far more valuable than the credit you will take for another's job well done.

As an example, think of what you notice and learn about the NFL quarterback who, when interviewed about winning the game, continues to point out that it was a team effort. Now compare and contrast that to the quarterback who takes the credit for the win. Which team would you rather be on? As a leader, I urge you to err on the side of caution here and make a commitment to always give credit to your team and employees. You will garner their respect and support, which in the long run is more important than the credit and will reflect well on you.

There is a time and a place to take credit and toot your own horn. That place is to your own manager and with regards to your own goals, objectives, and performance evaluation. I, like many of you, have a hard time patting myself on the back. I always err on the side of giving others credit. However, I make the exception when it comes to letting my boss know my accomplishments and the accomplishments of my team. There are times when, if you don't toot your horn, no one else will. Being confidently humble is finding balance between giving credit where credit is due and finding the time place to appropriately toot your own horn.

Recognize and honor the little people.

Your people are watching you and subconsciously they judge you on how you treat the little people. If you want to garner more respect and honor from your team and the people around you, treat the administrative and support staff with high regard. Don't get me wrong. I am not labeling the administrative and support staff "little people." My intent is to acknowledge that administrative and support staff often go unrecognized. I admonish leaders and managers to raise them up, respect them, honor them, and recognize them for the hard work they do.

Your team will see this and they will honor you for it. This includes the server at a business lunch, other drivers on the road, taxi drivers, janitors, and other maintenance people. This also includes people below you in the organization. When you are able to reach down and lift up those around you who typically don't get recognized, your employees and others will notice your humility.

Recently, I was meeting with the general manager of a large hotel in Chicago. We were on our way to meet with his executive staff and we were late. Along the way we encountered one of the housekeepers, who was having a hard time maneuvering her cleaning cart through the hallway. This general manager, although late to an important meeting, stopped to help the housekeeper. It didn't take long, but the fact that he stopped and helped was more telling about his character than anything I had heard him say. He was honoring the housekeeper by demonstrating through his actions that she was as important as the meeting he was about to attend.

Be teachable.

I mentioned earlier the importance of being an inspired leader – one who inspires others to reach higher and motivates employees to willingly donate their discretionary effort. You can also inspire, motivate, and build trust with others by being teachable. When the people around you believe that you are genuinely willing and able to learn, adapt, change for the better, and be inspired by them, there is a bond that is created. This is a bond of loyalty and dedication that will pay huge dividends.

Being teachable is more than listening, and it is not sitting in a meeting and agreeing with everything that is being said. It is the process by which you acknowledge you are teachable by learning from those around you and allowing yourself to be inspired. I have met far too many managers who are unwilling to consider that their employees may know more than they do and automatically dismiss a person and their ideas because of their title or job. If you allow it, you can learn from every person you encounter. And if you approach them with that attitude, you will be amazed at what you will discover.

Not that long ago I was coaching an executive of a large manufacturing shop. He was having difficulty with a few members of his immediate staff and wanted my help to resolve some issues. In my first session with this executive, he offered to give me a short tour of the shop floor. If you have ever been in a large manufacturing shop you know that they are noisy and often cluttered. But this was different.

Sure, it was loud from the machinery; but is was not cluttered. As I was given the tour, expecting a short ten to 15-minute walk through the shop, to my surprise it took most of the hour because this executive stopped and talked to the shop employees at every turn. He would stop, ask a question, and really listen to the answer. As I observed, I saw that this man, though he may have other faults, put himself in a position to learn from the people who did the work and saw the business from the ground floor and not the ivory tower.

What amazed me most is that he was asking for their opinions and *hearing* them. The tour finished, and I had a much better idea of what the problem with his managers might be. He expected them to be teachable, walk the talk, listen to the little people, and learn from them, too. He did this, but his immediate staff did not because they had become too busy and too important to take the time to listen and learn. Being teachable requires an investment. But that investment has a big pay-off.

Exercise appropriate vulnerability.

More often than not when I talk to my clients about being vulnerable, I can see that they are uncomfortable with this topic, particularly in a business or professional setting. There is still a stereotype of the white-collared executive who has no apparent Achilles' heel. There is a myth that in order to be successful as a manager, you need to be firm, bold, and "never let them see you sweat." When I speak of being vulnerable, I don't mean to contradict the need for boldness and confidence. But I believe you can stand your ground while also being appropriately vulnerable.

Several years ago, I was in a meeting where the general manager of a software division announced that the division would be closed and at least 50% of the division employees would be laid off. The general manager was visibly emotional and had tears in his eyes as he shared the bad news. Afterward he shared with me his embarrassment for having cried in front of the whole division. I was able to assure him that his emotions were exactly what was needed. His demonstration of vulnerability helped convey the message that he cared, that he was concerned about each employee, and that he was human.

Imagine the response if he had been hard, calloused, and unmoved. In this case, the general manager was appropriately vulnerable. Not so vulnerable that he wept on stage unable to keep his emotions in check; but he showed enough vulnerability at the right moment to demonstrate that he was both confident and humble. In the tough days that followed the announcement of the division closure, many employees commented on their general manager's display of emotions and how it helped them deal better with the difficulty of being laid off and more comfortably accept having to look for new employment.

Appropriate vulnerability is difficult to define. It is situation specific and does not always entail a visible demonstration of emotion. It is the ability to be real, to be human, and to be confident enough that mistakes will not paralyze you. I have met a lot of people who, when promoted to management and even executive level, felt as if they needed to leave their emotions at home and show a stoic face to the people. Appropriate vulnerability does not mean that you need to be everyone's best friend, nor does it mean that you allow yourself to be taken advantage of or stepped on.

It means that you will choose your battles and be unafraid to show your human side.

This supports the concepts in the section of this book about under-reacting. Freaking out is not appropriate vulnerability. Being vulnerable is the ability to allow yourself to feel upset, offended, hurt, or disrespected without flying off the handle. It also demonstrates that you are approachable and that people can confide in you.

Be quick to apologize.

When I work with organizations, I am often asked to meet with the employees of a manager or executive to assess their employees' perceptions and satisfaction. In the beginning, I was surprised at the amount of resentment within these organizations. I am no longer surprised. If you think there is no resentment among your employees or teams, you are seriously mistaken. Resentment is a trust-killer and will destroy your ability to lead.

Therefore, confident humility is also having the courage to apologize when you are wrong, which is also a demonstration of appropriate vulnerability. Quickly apologizing with sincerity and without strings is an effective way to diffuse resentment. Your apologies don't have to be elaborate speeches and don't necessarily need to be public apologies. But you can't dodge taking responsibility for your errors without creating resentment.

Learning to be vulnerable enough to apologize when warranted and doing it quickly will garner respect from your employees and motivate them to want to do more for you. It creates an environment of safety, which leads to greater performance. This also demonstrates that you own your mistakes (accountability) and will build trust instead of killing it, as I have described in the section on trust earlier in this book.

Being confidently humble requires you to be forgiving, refrain from holding grudges, and learn to let things go. Understand that by telling you to let things go, I don't mean letting mistakes go unnoticed or letting poor performance happen. What I mean is this: correct problems, forgive the people involved, and move on. Again, separate the person from the impact of the problem.

Throughout my career I have made mistakes, some of which were quite serious and costly. I was fortunate to have managers who forgave me and forgot about it and didn't hold it against me. Remember that resentment flows both ways — toward your employees from you, and toward you from your employees. Resentment is a trust-killer, and the sooner you eliminate resentment, the better leader you will be.

Being confidently humble allows you to be bold without arrogance. This enables you to have a greater influence on your employees and the people around you. Showing your human side with appropriate vulnerability will build trust, whereas condescension, disconnectedness, and harshness will only alienate others and breed resentment. The safer they feel, the more willing your employees will be to donate their discretionary effort.

Confident Humility In Review

No one likes arrogance, and no one wants to work for an arrogant manager. If you want to become a better leader, learn to be humble without sacrificing confidence — this is confident humility. Here are some ways to be confidently humble:

- Be generous in giving credit where credit is due. Don't give in to the temptation to take credit for your team's work because you are the leader or the manager. Acknowledge those whose efforts contributed to success. This is something that great leaders know how to do well.

- Honor and respect the little people. Treat all people around you with respect and honor – especially the support and administrative staff. This sends a clear message to your own employees that they are valuable to you, and you will reap the reward of more loyalty and dedication.

- Be teachable. Take the time to learn from those around you. As you do, you will demonstrate that they are important and that their ideas are valuable.

- Be appropriately vulnerable. This is a key aspect of great leaders – they know it is ok to be human, to make mistakes, and to show emotion. Don't be a robot! Let people see you for who you are.

- Be quick to apologize. Don't let bad feelings fester between you and your team. It is ok for a boss to make a mistake inadvertently; but then be quick to apologize to those whom you may have offended or hurt in some way.

Chapter 9:

Self-Discipline

While this may not be the longest section in the book, it is still an important part of becoming a better leader. As I have mentioned before, part of being a leader is just that – leading – meaning, being a person who others are willing to follow and willingly donate their discretionary effort. In other words, a true leader is *worthy* of inviting someone to follow your lead. So, ask yourself this: "Are you?"

Are you worthy of obtaining and retaining followers? I am not talking about the simple act of clicking a button on your Facebook app or accepting an invitation on LinkedIn – that is not the type of follower I am talking about. Followers are people who need vision, guidance, and support. Followers must willingly allow you to lead them.

Leadership is more than having a managerial or executive title, and it is more than having staff names below you on the org chart. It is even more than being the person who delivers an employee's performance evaluation. This is about your degree of character and the extent to which you can be trusted, flexible, insightful, resourceful, supportive, and visionary. To choose to follow you is a personal and emotional decision that someone else gets to make. A follower should require you to be someone worth following. You can become that person by increasing your self-discipline and practicing deferred gratification.

Last year I was called into work with the executive committee of a popular resort by their regional manager to help assess the effectiveness of the new general manager. The new general manager had been on the property for almost a year, and during those 12 months the morale and profit of the resort had declined. Complaints to the regional manager had increased. I interviewed the general manager's direct reports, as well as several key employees who, although they did not report directly to the general manager, interacted with him on a regular basis.

Through the various interviews I learned that the general manager was unequivocally qualified for the job. He had an illustrious resume and knew the hospitality business well. In Executive Committee meetings and with the leadership staff, he was professional and, for the most part, respectful. However, over the course of his first 12 months at this resort, the new general manager had developed the reputation of being a "partier."

His staff enumerated several occasions when the general manager had too much to drink and became "handsy" with the guests and the staff, as well as boisterous, rude, and condescending. He would even share his weekend escapades openly in staff meetings and with others. The executive committee was finding it hard to trust and respect him as a leader because they saw him as undisciplined, lacking self-control, and unprofessional. His established resume, business acumen, and his overall leadership effectiveness was being diminished because he had a reputation of losing control when he drank.

My report to the regional manager included the anecdotal stories of the general manager's misbehavior. When this was brought to the general manager's attention, his comment was, "What I do on my personal time is no one's business but mine." That may be true. But it did matter. He was hurting his relationships at work and losing trust and loyalty. His effectiveness as a leader was being questioned by his staff. Being a leader requires respect, and you garner respect from your team, employees, and direct staff by respecting yourself and others through exercising self-discipline. When it comes to being a better leader, respect trumps being the fun party guy.

Another example is that of Jeff, which is the fictitious pseudonym I will use for a real-life manager of a team of more than 150 service consultants – 75% men and 25% women. Jeff was well known in the industry and had a solid record of meeting goals and numbers. However, there was a growing resentment across his multi-state team, and I was asked to help Jeff overcome some negative comments in his 360-degree assessment.

When I met with Jeff, he dismissed the negative scores and comments in his assessment, believing that the comments were all from the women who reported to him. He felt it didn't matter since he consistently made is numbers.

The problem I uncovered had nothing to do with Jeff's overall management style. He was a strong businessman and quite knowledgeable about the issues faced by his consultants. He was also proud of how many hours in one-on-one meetings he held each month with his team. The problem was that most of those one-on-one meetings were held at strip clubs.

When questioned, many on his team members excused Jeff's behavior by saying that, "Jeff is just Jeff. He is harmless."

Well, it was not harmless. Other team members, male and female alike, felt that Jeff's choice of venue for meetings was undisciplined and inconsiderate. His persistent personal preference for having meetings in strip clubs eventually cost him his job. A little more self-discipline could have prevented him from getting fired.

Being disciplined does not mean you can't have fun or "party" with your team. It means that as a leader, whether you like it or not, you are held to a higher standard. As much as you want to be a friend, to be "one of the guys," or to be liked by everyone, you need to exercise more self-discipline than you might prefer.

This also means that you need to control your temper and manage your responses. Don't fly off the handle and don't be too easy on poor performers. Remember that it's about being worthy of respect. As you increase self-discipline you will garner more trust from your team, and they will be more willing to follow you.

Self-Discipline In Review

As you can imagine, no one wants to work for a sloppy or slovenly manager, and I don't mean only in appearance. I am referring especially to behavior. There are too many managers who feel they need to be "one of the boys," or "one of the girls," or to be liked. Leadership is not a popularity contest; it is a matter of earning respect. You will garner more respect by exercising self-discipline and self-mastery. This is something that some great leaders do naturally, and if you are one of them, congratulations. If not, this may be an area where you need to focus in order to become a better leader.

Chapter 10:

The Art of Macro-Management

The Art of Macro-Management is a key leadership principle that grew out of the endless reports of employees who resent their boss for being a micromanager. In all my years as a coach and a manager, I have only met one person who applauded his boss for being a micromanager. He loved that he didn't have to think about what to do. He depended on his boss to tell him what to do and how to do it. Certainly, this is not ideal for the employee or the boss, though.

Even with the overwhelming evidence that employees and staff don't like to be micromanaged, this management style continues to be prevalent in today's organizations. To my own surprise, I have met a few managers who laud the fact that they are micromanagers and wear it like a badge of honor. However, micromanagement is another trust-killer and minimizes employee effectiveness and job satisfaction.

At first blush you may think that macro-management is the opposite of micromanagement. I have found many websites and articles that will point that out. But great leaders know that macro-management is more than just not micromanaging. It is much more than simply taking a hands-off approach. Macro-management is a purposeful, strategic, and effective leadership style that can be applied to any organization and to any employee.

Not all employees are created equal. As a leader, your duty is to treat all employees fairly, but not necessarily the same. For example, new employees need more attention and direction than more tenured employees. It is absurd to think that you would treat them equally. Macro-management allows you to be attentive and directive to those who need it and less so to those who don't. Without exception, all employees want some level of attention from their boss. Some actually need their boss's attention to feel good about what they are doing. As a leader, don't confuse an employee's need for your attention as a justification to micromanage.

You may also think that without your detailed instructions or telling your employees how to do tasks, they will not get their job done or do it right. If that is the case, you have a different problem that should be addressed. If you have employees who cannot do their job or do it right without you micromanaging, then I would strongly suggest considering some significant changes that could include reorganizing staff, replacing employees, or providing more training. The broad truth is this: whenever there is micro-management, there is mistrust. Even the perception of micromanagement creates mistrust.

Macro-management does not mean turning your back and letting your employees do whatever they want, either. Managers who are not involved or don't show appropriate attention to their employees are not respected. As much as employees hate to be micromanaged, they also hate working for managers who don't care and don't pay attention.

When I start working with micromanagers to learn macro-management, the tendency for them is often to swing the pendulum all the way to becoming completely hands-off. Those managers quickly learn that laissez-faire management results in things getting out of control. They then fall back on their default style and micromanage things back under control.

I have found this particularly true with managers who were promoted from within and got the promotion because they were the best individual contributor, not because they had great management skills. Because they were a great individual contributor, they know the job well and could probably do the job better than the employees. Because they lack training in management skills, they usually resort to micromanagement as their default style.

Early in my career I was introduced to the concept of MBO – Management by Objectives. The MBO style of management was lauded at Hewlett Packard (HP) as the exceptional style of Bill Hewlett and Dave Packard, the founders. Indeed, Bill and Dave did manage by objective, and the HP Way had a strong component of MBO at its core.

Later, a version of this style of management was termed Management by Walking Around or MBWA. Personally, I appreciate both of these styles when they are used appropriately and not as a way of disguising micromanagement. Unfortunately, I have met plenty of managers who use MBWA and MBO as a means of exerting pressure on their staff and imposing their micromanaging style.

Management by Objective requires work and skills to set proper objectives, as well as coaching to help employees develop skills necessary to understand and meet those objectives. But most managers have a hard time leaving it to objectives and resort to a form of MMBO – Microman-agement by Objective.

Consider macro-management a derivative or style of MBO, but as MBO at its best. Macro-management can be applied to all employees regardless of their experience and tenure. It can be used for new employees just learning their jobs, who may need a bit more attention and guidance, as well as for seasoned employees who don't need guidance as much as they need support and confidence that you have their backs.

Macro-management is embodied in this short simple phrase: expect the best, accept the rest, and mildly neglect. First let me cover 'expect the best.'

Expect the Best

This part of the phrase reminds us that we should expect the best from the people who work for us and from the people around us. Employees have a keen sense of what you expect from them. While they may not know the exact expectations from a step-by-step perspective, they instinc-tively know if you expect the best from them or have low-ered your expectations.

When someone does not live up to what we expect of them, it is natural to lower our expectations. In lower-ing those expectations, we send a signal that we are dis-appointed in them. Lowering expectations is a dangerous, slippery slope that sends a strong message to the other employees, as well. This often creates a fear-based environ-ment that is neither emotionally safe nor healthy and is counterproductive.

I have coached hundreds of managers and executives who address poor performance by lowering expectations and standards as part of a performance improvement plan. While I believe that you don't need to treat every employee the same, it is imperative that you don't lower expectations. You may want to change an employee's job description to include fewer responsibilities, which I will talk about next. But even in that case, you should still expect the best from that employee.

Your employees should know that you expect the best from them and that they will be assessed on how well they perform against those expectations. Expecting the best should imply to your employees that you believe in them and that you have their backs. Often in one-on-one coaching sessions I ask my clients who in their past believed in them. Many will say an athletic coach, a high-school teacher, and some will say a former manager.

When I ask what made them think that this person believed in them, most have answered that this person expected the best from them and then helped them achieve it. You can do the same for your employees. Don't lower your expectations. Keep them high. Focus instead on helping them meet those expectations. You can start doing that by accepting what they can do; in other words, focus on the next part of the slogan of macro-management – accept the rest.

Accept the Rest

Accepting the rest, as the motto says, means you will accept what an employee can give, and what they can do, as well as what their strengths are. The reason I focus on 'acceptance' is because it is the opposite of denial. Far too many managers will either lower their expectations or actually reject an employee when they don't meet their expectations. Rather than lowering your expectations or rejecting the employee, accept them where they are, at their present performance level, and then step in as a coach to help them improve.

I am strong believer in a coaching approach to management. Most employees are open to coaching when performed not as a task-master, drill sergeant, or slave master, but like a true coach. One that will assess an employee's performance and then help them do better and excel. This will require you to have an open and honest relationship with your employees, where performance is an open topic discussed regularly and not just during their annual performance review.

Imagine that you wanted to become a better runner. Perhaps you would like to become a marathon runner, and so you hire a running coach. The first thing the coach will do is assess your current performance, running style, training regiment, and even your equipment, such as shoes. A true coach would then accept that level of performance and use it as a baseline for improvement.

That improvement will come in the form of insights from experience, tips, best practices, knowledge, and skill of the coach. If the running coach was sincerely interested in improving performance, he would not lower his expectations but accept what you could give and invest in you becoming better. Both expecting the best and accepting the rest are keys to macro-management. The next step in becoming an excellent macro-manager is to mildly neglect.

Mild neglect is adopted from Management by Objective. In order to rise above micromanagement and take a macro approach, you need to step back and, to an appropriate degree, give your employees latitude. Now, this may run counterintuitive to all of the management literature that says you must be attentive and involved with your employees; and to a large extent, I agree.

However, employees want to have a high degree of independence. They want to show you that they can meet your expectations. They want to be left alone to do their work. This requires some courage on your part to step back and let your employees succeed or fail on their own. This doesn't mean that you ignore them, and this doesn't mean that you don't pay attention to them. In this context, the principle of "neglect" means to give them the rope they need, latitude, as well as your support, communicating to your employees that you have their backs and want them to succeed. When they succeed on their own, their success is that much sweeter. And their success makes you successful.

Watch any professional sports game and you will see that when the opening buzzer sounds or the whistle blows, the coach is not on the court or the field with the players. Any good coach knows that at game time, he will be on the sidelines. Take your appropriate role on the sidelines of the game with some mild neglect.

Mildly Neglect

Macro-management is to expect the best, accept the rest, and mildly neglect. Macro-management will require you to prepare your team. They need to know what the objectives are, what the context of their job is, and why they do what they are getting paid to do. They need to what your expectations are and what is required of them. They need to know and feel that you have their backs and support them. There will need to be a high degree of trust in order for macro-management to be effective, and I highly recommend that you study and implement the skills in this book, as they will enable you to implement macro-management.

This leads me to the final topic of macro-management – how to deal with failure. Earlier in this section I recommended that your employees need some rope by which to succeed or fail on their own. This will require you to become more comfortable with failure. When I speak to this in a public forum, I get some strange looks from those who have a hard time accepting failure and believe that failure is not an option. If that is your approach to failure, then chances are you will be disappointed because failure is par for the course when it comes to achieving success.

Many would consider Michael Jordan to be one of the world's best basketball players. Even today, after Michael Jordan has been out of the game for more than a decade, great players are still compared to him. However, Michael Jordan has failed! He failed many times in his life and in his career. Michael even admitted this when he said, "I've missed more than 9,000 shots in my career. I've lost almost 300 games. Twenty-six times I've been trusted to take the game-winning shot and missed. I've failed over and over and over again in my life. And that is why I succeed" (Goldman & Papson, 1998).

By his own admission Michael Jordan says that his success involved trying and failing over and over again. I also appreciate this same mindset of Orville Redenbacher, icon of the world's best popping corn. As many of you know, it was Orville's life's passion and work to create the world's best popping corn, and over his long career he tried more than 10,000 different recipes before he found what he considered to be the best. In his own words he said, "I didn't fail once because each time I learned what not to do" (Sherman, 1996).

In order for macro-management to work you need to redefine failure to mean success. It is a success if you can learn what not to do. Even more so, it is a success if you can help your employees learn what not to do and help them do it better the next time, rather than stand over their shoulder telling them every little step so that failure is not an option.

One of the most important lessons I learned in my career came from a significant failure. In the early 1990s, I was the product manager for a new HP Laserjet – the first laser-jet printer to have a vertical paper feed and to be in the sub-$500 price category. This was an important product for Hewlett Packard with expectations that this new printer would break previous records and expand the Laserjet brand into geographies such as India and China that were extremely price sensitive.

Part of my job was to write the product plan that would serve as the guide to the printer's target customer, geographies, features, competition, and financials. I had never done a product plan before and understood a product plan to mean a series of PowerPoint slides to cover each of the topics in the plan. My manager at the time had very high expectations and coached me on the overall parts of the plan. However, when I first presented the product plan to management, I was bombarded with questions that I could not answer; nor were they covered in the product plan. The plan itself was rejected, and I felt rejected as well.

At first I was angry that my manager did not prepare me for the meeting with management and did not give me detailed instructions on what a product plan should look like – especially that it should be more of a full-blown detailed report and not just conjecture on slides. However, that failure and my manager's subsequent coaching incentivized me to meet her high expectations.

Ultimately, I wrote a product plan that was used from that point on as the example of what a product plan should be for many HP Laserjets that followed. My manager expected the best, accepted what I could give, and then mildly neglected. I learned more through that process and felt better about the overall outcome than I would have if she had micromanaged me to death to write the plan exactly how SHE wanted it.

Let me relate this to the previous example of wanting to become a better runner. With high expectations and accepting your current level of running, the coach will then stand by and watch you run the race. He will not jump in when you feel tired and run for you, nor will he run beside you to give you step-by-step (no pun intended) instructions along the way. He will advise and admonish as necessary, as well as observe ways for you to improve.

Macro-management will pay off. It can help you become a better leader by freeing you from all of the time and energy it takes to micromanage a team. Moving from micromanaging to macro-managing will not happen overnight. I recommend that you start by focusing on the formula to build trust and let macro-management become a natural outcome of trusting yourself and then building trust within your team, as well as employing the other powerful concepts in this book to help you become a better leader.

You can be a better leader! Just as with all of the skills presented in this book, macro-management requires balance and effort. It becomes more effective as the previous skills in this book are learned and implemented.

Macro-Management In Review

Don't be a micromanager! I have seen this kill the enthusiasm of great teams and create resentment. Great leaders know how to macro-manage. You, too, can become a macro-manager by learning and living this concept: expect the best, accept the rest, and mildly neglect. Many people don't like the word 'neglect,' as it sounds negative and tends to imply negligence. I am not advocating negligence in any way. I am advocating that you refrain from being a control-freak. Step back, let your team succeed or fail appropriately, and help them learn from their mistakes and make failure a success. This is not done in a vacuum, and there may be people on your team who need more training and help before you can mildly neglect.

Conclusion

If you have come to this part of the book either having read through to this point or by jumping ahead, I am grateful you had the interest and invested in yourself and your career. As I mentioned in the introduction, this is not meant to be an academic discussion on leadership, or another book based on studies and research, but a 'how-to' book written conversationally, focused on real-world practical skills that work. Whether you are just starting your career or are a seasoned manager, you can be a better leader now!

Whether you are an aspiring leader or currently managing an organization, you can learn to inspire your team to more willingly donate their discretionary effort and eagerly follow you with more loyalty and dedication. This does not mean you need to change who you are or alter your personality. In fact, I would strongly suggest you don't do that, but use the skills in this book to augment and amplify your natural gifts, talents, and strengths to become a better leader.

I am realistic and practical enough to recognize that not every skill or concept in this book will appeal to you; but I am hoping that, as with most books, you will find many nuggets of wisdom and insight that you will be able to put into practice immediately. I have taught and coached these skills for more than 25 years with tremendous success, and it has always humbled me when a client will come to a session having implemented some of the skills in this book with great success.

Recently, I ran into a client who had completed the *Be a Better Leader NOW!* coaching program a year ago. He was thrilled to report that he had been promoted, not once, but twice! He attributed his promotions, neither of which he applied for but was asked to accept, to what he had learned in our sessions. And most of what he had learned is what I have included in this book.

In the past 12 months more than 50% of my clients have been promoted, given awards such as "Leader of the Year," or found new jobs with higher pay and better opportunities. These skills really do work. Please don't take my word for it. Try them out and see for yourself.

Be a Better Leader NOW! has been purposely organized as a roadmap to help you become a better leader or manager or to acquire new skills that will help you become promotable and a better individual contributor. This roadmap has been designed to take you from the most fundamental skill of developing and maintaining trust to adapting and exercising the Art of Macro-Management. While each skill and chapter can stand on its own, the sequence is important, as well. Here is the roadmap in brief:

1. **The Trust Advantage**: Trust is the Sine Qua Non of leadership. Meaning that, without it, everything else you try or do will be minimized or ineffective. Without trust, leading and managing will require a brute force effort, and your team and employees will work out of duty and likely do it with resentment. Trust gives you an advantage personally, professionally, organizationally,

and financially. Remember the T.R.U.S.T. formula to build and maintain a high degree of trust.

2. **The Optimist's Advantage**: Optimism is not something you are just born with. It can be learned and taught. As you become more optimistic from a foundation of trust, your team will be more willing to donate their discretionary effort and follow you. Optimists have an advantage: they make more money, close more deals, enjoy better health, and have better relationships. I have only covered a few of the many ways to acquire greater optimism, so look for my book *The Optimist's Advantage* for more practical skills to enhance your optimism and reap the advantage.

3. **It's All About the WHO**: People are the key to your success as a leader. You become a better leader by realizing that numbers, metrics, and data are important but mean nothing without the people who actually do the work. In every encounter or conversation there are three things present: facts, feelings, and needs. Refuse to talk about facts until you understand the feelings and needs of the people involved. That includes how they feel about the facts and the data. This becomes so much easier as you build trust and are viewed as an optimist.

4. **The Art of Appreciation**: This skill works magic. While that may seem bold, it is true. In fact, I may be *understating* the positive impact this can have on your team and the people with whom you associate. Don't be afraid to appreciate the people who work for you and with you. Remember that praise is about what they do, and appreciation is about who they are. Everyone

wants to be seen for who they are. Recognizing and appreciating them for their good character traits will add depth to the trust you have built, as well as help them become more optimistic and experience that they are important as a person, and not just for what they do.

5. **Context, Context, Context**: Why do your people come to work? If they come to work just for a paycheck, you will have problems. Help your employees and the people around you recognize their purpose and the meaning of their job. When an employee has purpose and knows the meaning and the context of what they are doing and why, they are even more willing to donate their discretionary effort. If you don't know the context, then learn it so that your employees can internalize it.

6. **The Art of Disclaimers**: Learning to disclaim your motive, intention, objective, and mood will strengthen all of your relationships and help you become a better communicator. It builds greater trust and helps people feel they are important. Disclaimers help with decision making and dealing with tough topics and situations. This also allows people to see you as real and human and takes the guesswork out of dealing with you. Using disclaimers builds trust, supports your ability to appreciate, and focuses on the people instead of the facts. It allows you to express your feelings and needs, rather than focus on facts alone. The Art of Disclaimers is one of the most powerful skills included in this book.

7. **Authentic Curiosity**: You will recall that curiosity is not about being nosey or meddling. It is an expression of care and demonstrates that you are interested

in someone, especially when it is authentic and not overused. Being curious is a skill of great leaders; they know what questions to ask and how to ask them in a way that gets people to open up and comfortably say more than they intended to say. You can imagine how much more powerful authentic curiosity is when built on a foundation of trust, focusing on the 'who' (and not just the 'what'), having appreciated and praised your employees, and disclaiming your motive and intent.

8. **Confident Humility**: No one likes working for an arrogant boss. Arrogance is a trust-killer and minimizes all of the skills included in this book. Being confidently humble does not mean you are weak or demure. It is about being more interested in others than in yourself and giving credit where credit is due. Leaders who are viewed as both confident and humble have a distinct advantage in that people will confide in them, trust them, and have their back. Confident humility supports, substantiates, and lifts all of the other skills included here.

9. **Discipline and Deferred Gratification:** Undisciplined leaders (those who can't control themselves, their mouths, and who misbehave) don't garner the trust and respect that great leaders do. Raising your level of self-discipline includes making and keeping promises and confidences, which will help you maintain trust and inspire your employees to donate their discretionary effort. Flying off the handle, partying hard, coming in late, and sloppy work are all indicators of an undisciplined leader. A lack of discipline is a trust-killer, destroys optimism, and reduces the impact

of praise and appreciation. Self-discipline does not mean that you analyze everything to the nth degree and become ultra-conservative. Overdoing self-discipline can lead to micromanagement of self that will bleed over into how you manage others.

10. **The Art of Macro-Management:** The final stop along the roadmap of becoming a better leader is to learn the Art of Macro-Management. You may be tempted to jump to this skill immediately because it is powerful and effective. However, macro-management is much more effective when based on the foundation of the other nine skills in this book. This skill is epitomized in this phrase: expect the best, accept the rest, and mildly neglect. Expecting the best is easier and more effective when implemented by a disciplined leader, one who appreciates employees, is optimistic, disclaims intentions and motives, and is confidently humble. Accepting the rest is based on a foundation of trust and focuses on the 'who' (not just the 'what') and applies authentic curiosity and self-discipline. Mild neglect cannot be given without trust, disclaiming your intentions and objectives, and focusing on people more than mere facts or data.

These ten skills and concepts are your roadmap to becoming a better leader now! They will also help you in every aspect of your life and in all of your relationships. For more than 15 years I have worked from a home office located downstairs near my living room and kitchen. Often my wife overheard me speaking to my team, participating in conference calls, and talking to customers. One day, several years ago, she came into my office and asked me,

"Why don't you talk to me the same way you talk to your employees?"

At first I was defensive, but then I reflected on what she had asked. I realized that I was somewhat of a different person at work than when I was at home, and that the same skills I used at work to be a better leader could help me be a better man, husband, and father.

The good news is that becoming a better person requires learning and developing the same skills necessary to be a better leader. I didn't need to learn a new skill set to help me in other aspects of my life. I just needed to be more conscientious about using the skills at home and away from work. These same skills will improve your life, just as they did mine. Consequently, I also started to use these skills with individual clients who come to me for personal and relationship issues with great success, as well.

All of my clients know that I love to have the last word – one last tidbit of counsel or guidance – before I end each session. Let me do the same here by giving you a final admonition that will enable all of the above skills, and that is this – don't hire jerks! As much as you may be tempted to overlook how a candidate fits into your team because they have an impressive resume of experience, don't hire them if you discern that they are difficult! It is much harder to change someone's attitude, mannerisms, personality, and demeanor than it is to teach them skills and processes of what the job entails. Hiring jerks will thwart your efforts to be a better leader.

I am not advocating that you hire candidates, friends, family, or people who are exactly like you. I am however, strongly suggesting that you assess how a candidate will get along with you, your team, and other associates, and whether or not they will be an optimistic addition to the group. Assess how wiling they are to trust and be trusted. Assess who they are, not just what they do. If you take the Art of Appreciation seriously, then consider what you would appreciate about a candidate. I have been duped, and many great managers I know have been duped, by excellent interviewers. As you learn and apply the skills in this book, I hope that you become better at interviewing and assessing potential candidates. Remember to consider their fit over function.

Now, a word regarding existing employees who may be jerks. As a wise leader once told me, "Sometimes in order to change the people, you need to change the people." I have had jerks who worked for me, and it consumed my energy and minimized my efforts to become a better leader. Don't let that happen to you. If you have jerks on your team, help them to help themselves by giving them the opportunity to change (you might consider using a praise sandwich) or inspire them to advance their career through another opportunity in another company or organization. You will do them and yourself a great service.

Bonus Chapter:

Self-Worth, Esteem, and Confidence

What you do

Self-Confidence

Self-Esteem

Self-Worth

Who you are – personal significance

Becoming a better leader has more to do with who you are than what you do. The previous chapters in this book create a roadmap of skills and concepts that when applied and practiced will help you become a great leader. The effectiveness and power of those skills relies upon, in part, your self-worth. What follows is a section from my book *I AM STRONG* to help you understand and discover how to increase your self-worth and use it as a foundation to become a better leader.

In any discussion about self-worth, self-esteem, and self-confidence, I am invariably asked about the difference between self-worth and self-esteem. After looking long and hard and reading several books and scientific studies, I have not found satisfying definitions. So rather than cite definitions that I don't wholly agree with, I would prefer to describe them by introducing you to what I call the Self-Worth Pyramid.

As you can see in the graphic, self-worth is the largest component and can be considered the foundation of the pyramid. Self-confidence is the smallest component and is found at the top. Self-confidence is important and should not be disregarded but has less importance and less significance than self-worth and self-esteem. Let me explain.

Self-worth is more about who you are and is determined by how inherently worthy you feel. It has a strong component of personal significance and is mostly an internal phenomenon. You are considered to have high self-worth when you have a deep knowledge that by just being here, you make a difference; that your life is having a positive impact on the world around you.

Your self-worth is not determined by anything external, such as compliments and accolades. It is an internal knowledge of who you are regardless of your external circumstances. Self-worth is strongly associated with your beliefs about yourself. While self-worth is not about your achievements, it is about spending energy and effort in pursuits that are meaningful to you.

When you feel worthy, you feel motivated to make behavior choices that support your overall goals of success and joy. Self-worth should be a baseline of worthiness that can never diminish based on your situation or external circumstances. Self-worth can only grow, and later in this section I will share several things you can start doing right now to create a foundation of self-worth that cannot shrink, but only expand.

Self-confidence, on the other hand, is about what you do and is mostly developed from external sources, such as compliments and achievements, and it is dependent on situations and circumstances. Think of self-confidence as a byproduct of self-worth and self-esteem. I have found that many people focus on their self-confidence and then complain that they are not getting the results they had hoped for. The reason is that there is only so much gain you can get from improving your self-confidence. That is especially true if you have not taken the time to establish true self-worth and grown your self-esteem.

The small triangle at the top of the pyramid represents the limited return on investment you get from increased self-confidence. Don't get me wrong. Self-confidence is important and should not be minimized. For instance, I feel much more confident speaking in front of an audience when I have a fresh haircut. Perhaps you have experienced this, as well, by wearing your favorite dress or best suit for a job interview. This happens to all of us and it is an important thing to consider. Maybe you have experienced greater confidence when you are fully prepared or have practiced well. My wife is a musician, and I know she feels more confident for a performance when she has practiced adequately. You see, self-confidence is about what you do.

How you feel about what you can do is an external factor in how you feel about yourself. Let me tell you a personal story as an example. It wasn't that long ago that I attempted to fulfill a life-long dream of learning to play the piano. It was fortunate that there was a willing teacher in our neighborhood, which made taking lessons quite convenient. As I began to learn piano, I found that it was both easier and more difficult than I had anticipated. My biggest problem was timing and rhythm.

When it came time for a recital, I was beside myself with nervousness that completely surprised me. I am generally at home in front of an audience and quite confident in my ability to speak and convey a message. However, when it came to playing the piano, it was quite the opposite. My self-confidence varies based on the circumstances, as I am sure yours does, as well. This is in contrast to self-worth, which is not circumstantial and should not change with the situation.

Self-esteem is between self-confidence and self-worth and can be best described as thoughts about what you can do because of who you are. I am not going to spend a lot of time on self-esteem because I believe the best course of action is to invest in your self-worth, which will have a direct result on your self-esteem and your self-confidence.

Self-esteem is not something you were born with; it is something you have learned. In fact, growing your self-esteem has more to do with un-learning low self-esteem behaviors than it does about learning how to have high self-esteem. Again, later in this chapter you will learn a few skills that will help you un-learn low self-esteem behavior.

The reason why this distinction is so important (self-confidence is about WHAT YOU DO and self-worth is about WHO YOU ARE) is that we too often confuse the two. For instance, when we are criticized about something we have 'done,' it's easy to interpret it as a criticism of who we are. Let me use this example. I am sure that many of you have or have had children in school, and, at one time or another, that child brought home a report card with lower grades than your child was capable of achieving. What was your reaction?

I am sure you realized that the number one reason for getting a bad grade has nothing to do with your child's level of intelligence. What is the number one cause of bad grades? Poor effort! Most often grades are a reflection of effort rather than the result of being unintelligent. So, in an attempt to counsel your child, you try to help them realize that they are smart enough to get good grades but need to put in better effort.

Many times this turns into a fight or some type of argument. Why? The reason is that your child, as many of us have done in the same situations, is confusing something they have DONE with WHO THEY ARE. As hard as you try to be specific about the effort needed to get good grades, your child will likely interpret your comments as telling them they are not smart enough.

We do the same thing. I have seen this over and over again with my clients when they interpret criticism and rejection as demeaning who they are – letting the negative comments flow down into the bottom of the pyramid – instead of keeping the feedback at the top of the pyramid and letting it be about something they have done. We need to realize this ourselves and help our children realize the distinction between something we do and who we are.

Steve came to my office determined that he was a bad person and asked me to help him overcome his issues with self-confidence. After some discussion I learned that Steve had completely confused his notions of self-worth and self-confidence. He certainly was not a bad person; but indeed, he had made some bad choices and was suffering the consequences of those choices. It only took a few sessions for Steve to start to see that what you DO does not determine who you are, and that although he had made some bad choices, that does not make him a bad person.

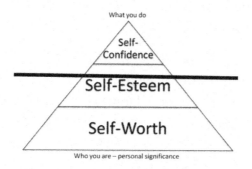

One of the most important things you can do is to draw a line, a hard and fast line, right across the middle of the self-worth pyramid that represents a hard boundary, so that you do not let any criticism about what you have done flow down to have an impact on who you are. Imagine the power this will have in your life!

The Vicious Cycle of Low Self-Worth

Most people lump all of their self-worth and self-confidence issues into one bucket and come to the conclusion that they have low self-esteem. The question becomes, how do you know? How do you know if you have low self-esteem, low self-confidence, or low self-worth? Having low self-worth and self-confidence is a lot like bad breath – it is much easier to detect in others than it is to detect in ourselves.

Low self-worth can be described as having a low opinion of yourself and feelings of being unworthy. The biggest problem with believing you have, or acting as if you have, low self-worth is that you behave according to that belief, and the very act reinforces your belief, creating a vicious cycle that is difficult to break. It is usually in the midst of this cycle that a client will come to see me for help.

Low self-worth is at the core of most of the problems that my clients come to me to help solve. It affects every aspect of our life. From a job interview to an argument with your child or spouse or a family dispute, low self-worth causes seemingly small issues to become exaggerated and worse than they really are.

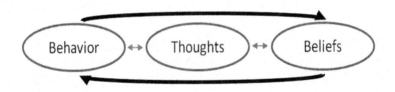

If you believe you are unworthy of love, you will act as though you are unworthy of love. If you believe you are an outcast, you will act as if you are an outcast. Your beliefs define your reality. In truth, you are so much more than what you believe about yourself. These beliefs, who you believe you are, when created from a position of low self-worth generate what I call mistaken certainties. These mistaken certainties, invalid beliefs about ourselves, limit the joy and happiness we can feel, as well as the fulfillment we could feel in our relationships and in most everything we do.

Brad came to me with what he considered a major problem. He was falling in love with a blond. At first I almost laughed until he explained that every other woman that he had dated with blond hair had dumped him. He really loved this woman but could not get past the fact that she was blond and, like the others, would surely dump him. You may think this ridiculous, but to Steve it was as real as having anxiety about going to the dentist or being afraid of heights. He came to me insecure, unsure of what to do, and he felt that he was no good around blonds. Brad was operating under a mistaken certainty; and though our nemesis may not be blond women, it is likely something else that we needlessly allow to minimize our self-worth.

Another example is someone who might say they are no good at math. What does it mean that someone is not good at math? Does it mean they are incapable of balancing their checkbook or that they can't remember how to calculate the area of a circle? Does it mean they can't figure out the price of something on sale at 15% discount or that they can't convert gallons into liters?

To make a statement of final judgment like, "I am no good at math," is a mistaken certainty. It is not a statement about WHO YOU ARE but a statement about what you can or cannot DO. There is a difference and you need to be careful to not confuse the two and create a self-image based on mistaken certainties that limit your ability to be happy, to enjoy new experiences, and to feel satisfied and content.

The Upside of Low Self-Worth

Every motivational speaker and thousands of authors will tell you how bad it is to have a low self-worth and low self-esteem. If it is all that bad, why do we put up with it? Could there be any upside to feeling worthless? You may think I am being sarcastic, when, in truth, I am asking an honest question. Feeling helpless and feeling worthless can be a safe option because you protect yourself from the pain you might suffer when things go wrong or the pain from rejection of any kind.

For example, if you already know you are no good, then it doesn't hurt as bad when no one will hire you or care enough to listen to you. If you already feel you are not worthy of being loved, then when rejection comes your way, as it does for all of us, you are validated because you knew it was going to happen anyway. Feeling helpless can be misconstrued as a safe way to face the failure, adversity, and trials that come to all of us. In some strange way this person is actually validated by the bad things that happen because they felt that way already.

Another safe option for people who feel worthless is that they don't have the burden of even trying to succeed in anything that matters because there's simply no point. If you act as if what you say or feel is worthless, then people leave you alone and don't ask for your opinion or participation. Because you do not have to be responsible for anything, you avoid having to be accountable to anyone. Or so it seems.

People who feel that they have no valuable skills or talents may feel safe because no one will ask them to apply them. When you say you are useless, hopeless, and a failure, then people lower their expectations of you to the point of not having any expectations at all. You can live a life free of the expectations of others. This can be your way of getting sympathy and attention, and you can sit back in your safe cocoon waiting for someone to come and rescue you from your safe place of worthlessness.

For some of you, this may be all you know. Perhaps you have lived with feelings of inadequacy and unworthiness for so long, you don't know any better and you have think this is just the way you are. Feeling worthless, unworthy, and helpless has become your normal. But know this: you are not your programming; you are not what others have said about you. *You are so much more.* It's time to create a new normal, a normal that is full of hope, power, and feelings of being worthy of success, love, and fulfillment.

If you suffer from low self-worth and self-esteem, you also suffer from low self-confidence, which can have an effect on most aspects of your life. Here are some of the things that you will experience:

- Over-sensitivity – being easily offended; feeling others are judging you
- Need/desire for praise
- Constantly seeking external validation
- Boasting, bragging, and judging others
- Feeling stupid, fat, ugly, useless, or unwanted
- A sense of not being good enough or on equal ground with others
- Not feeling strong enough to handle things on your own
- Needing to be more articulate, prettier, smarter, richer, etc.
- Finding it hard to forgive yourself for making mistakes
- Dissatisfaction with life
- Depression

- Low energy levels
- Feeling helpless to change things
- Feeling stuck
- Feeling either superior or inferior to others, never equal
- Withdrawn from social contact
- A sense of defeat and hopelessness

The Formula to High Self-Worth: I AM STRONG

Deep down, all of us WANT to feel valued – and so we spend much of our lives searching for significance. We search for the feeling of being important and significant in the things we do and the people we are with. We search for significance in the job we have and the contributions we make. All of those things can be good and certainly have their place, but you don't need to search any longer.

All the significance you need is already within you! You are just like the characters in *The Wizard of Oz*, who each had what they needed all along without getting it from anyone or anything. All the significance you are searching for, all the validation you need, all the worthiness you need to feel is within you and can be accessed through the formula to high self-worth, represented by the letters in this easy to remember sentence: I AM STRONG!

Let me first share the benefits of I AM STRONG and then help you learn this powerful formula. As you have been reading this, you may have already thought of someone you know who has high self-worth and high self-esteem. You may also have someone in mind who demonstrates an abundance of self-confidence to the point of being boastful or prideful. People with true, genuine, real, sincere self-worth, however well-known they are, usually display different characteristics than someone who has high self-confidence. Think of someone you know whom you consider to have high self-worth. You may recognize some of these characteristics:

- Quiet confidence and sense of security
- No need to prove themselves to others
- Comfortable with silence and comfortable alone
- Do not fish for compliments - but they do accept them well
- Demonstrate humility
- Listen well to others
- Recognize others and give credit where credit is due
- External recognition is secondary to internal satisfaction

You can read the body language of someone with high self-worth, as it usually speaks louder than what they may be saying. They are often physically relaxed, upright, calm, and measured in movement; they are decisive without hesitation and make good eye contact freely and comfortably.

The I AM STRONG formula will create enormous benefits in every aspect of your life. Sure, it is easy to focus on the negative side effects of low self-worth, but I think it is important that you also understand that there are enormous benefits to taking steps to improve the health of your self-worth. Below are some of the benefits you can expect as you learn and practice the I AM STRONG formula. These benefits are further experienced by using the skills presented in each part of the formula and are reinforced in the accompanying audio course. You will...

- Become optimistic!
- Learn to like and love yourself
- Behave with a sense of purpose
- Forgive easier
- Enjoy better health
- Become wealthier
- Develop better and more fulfilling relationships
- Respond better to medical treatments
- Cope with and handle change better
- Grow your self-esteem
- Grow your self-confidence
- Know that you are worthy of all the good that life has to offer → happiness, love, success, and fulfillment
- Gain a deep KNOWLEDGE that you make a difference in this world.

Before I begin to explain the I AM STRONG formula, it is important to note that feeling worthy is different from feeling you deserve recognition, reward, or validation. The word "deserve" represents some form of reciprocation, or a feeling that you should get something because you have done something good, have sacrificed something or suffered in some way, or because others have what you want that you are owed. Self-worth is not about deserving anything. It is a feeling of worthiness that emanates from the inside, knowing that you are inherently worthy just because you are.

This becomes another important distinction because we are bombarded with messages that we are entitled to greatness, good things, big cars, big houses, or some kind of accolades because of something we do. Some people serve others and feel good about it, as long as it is recognized and they are acknowledged in some way. High self-worth does not demand recognition and does not require accolades. High self-worth is a strong sense of self based on an internal knowledge that you are good and valued, even if no one says so.

I AM STRONG - Your Formula for High Self-Worth

High self-worth creates inner strength that comes from a strong sense of worthiness. You feel inherently worthy of all that you dream of, all that you desire, as well as true, enduring happiness. Your will experience greater self-esteem and confidence. What used to bother and offend you will no longer be an issue. You will find inner strength to handle change, adversity, and drama better. The I AM STRONG formula is a nine-step formula that is built on practical skills that will help you shed feelings of low self-worth and empower you to see yourself as a wonderful, capable, strong person. Here is the formula in a nutshell:

I is for Identify

For many of us, we don't spend a lot of time dwelling on the health of our self-worth. It is so easy to blame others for our lack of confidence and low self-esteem that we rarely take a good look at ourselves to realize that we are much more capable of defining our happiness and significance than we realize. In this step of the formula you start to look at yourself differently to see if your self-worth needs an overhaul.

A is for Awareness, Acceptance, and Acknowledge

Once you identify the health of your self-worth it is important to become aware of what triggers your responses and how you react in certain situations. You do this through observation, acceptance, and acknowledgement. Without accepting yourself, your circumstances, your weakness and strengths without self-indictment, you remain in denial, unable to move forward. You cannot change what you do not accept and acknowledge. In this step you will begin to see yourself for the great person you are and start to lose dependence on others to build you up and validate you.

M is for Minimize your weaknesses and Maximize your strengths

It is unfortunate that we are much more acquainted with our weaknesses than our strengths and believe that our weaknesses far outweigh our strengths and talents. In this step in the formula to create high self-worth you need to take the weaknesses you accept and acknowledge in the previous step and minimize them as you maximize your strengths.

S is for Self-Recognition

Your self-worth is on shaky ground if you are dependent on validation from others to affirm your worth. Validation from others is inconsistent and can often be insincere as people will tell you what you want to hear rather than the truth. In this step of the formula, you will learn the power of self-recognition and validation to cure your dependence on others.

T is for being Trustworthy

Low self-worth is often exhibited by not trusting your own decisions, intuition and needs. As your self-worth increases, you will become more confident in your own decision making, as well as grow in your ability to handle life's challenges to the best or your ability and refrain from making emotional trade-offs.

R is for Respecting your needs

We all have emotional needs. For many, those needs are secondary to the needs and emotions of others. There is a fine balance between serving others and self-care. To provide the best and most appropriate service to others in the various roles you play, you must express your needs, stop comparing yourself to others, and become more assertive. This doesn't mean you will be unreasonable or become an emotional bully but that you will learn how to prioritize self-care.

O is for Own it!

Becoming responsible and accountable for your own emotions, thoughts, feelings, and behavior is a critical part of the I AM STRONG formula. As you become emotionally accountable you stop blaming others for your misfortune. And as you stop blaming others, you are no longer a victim but can lead your own life.

N is for Nourish

Your self-worth is a living thing. Without consistent and positive nourishment, your self-worth will wither away like a plant without water. In this step, you will learn the power of creating a criticism filter, as well as how to preserve, protect, and affirm your great worth.

G is for Genuine

High self-worth requires you to live authentically and with integrity. This comes about by aligning what you now believe about yourself (having adopted the first eight steps) with your thoughts and actions. When this happens, you significantly reduce the inner conflict that is present with low-self worth. Becoming genuine is also a benefit of high self-worth.

The I AM STRONG formula to build and maintain a high self-worth can be found in detail in the book *I AM STRONG: The Formula to Build Your Self-Worth from the Inside Out*. Also in that book are several sections to further improve your life, peace, and happiness.

Bibliography

Achor, S. (2010). *The Happiness Advantage*. New York: Crown Publishing Group.

Collins, J., & Hansen, M. T. (2011). *Great by Choice*. New York: Harper Collins Publishers.

Covey, S. M. (2006). *The Speed of Trust*. New York: Covey-Link LLC.

Covey, S. R. (1989, 2004). *The 7 Habits of Highly Effective People*. New York: Free Press, A Division of Simon & Schuster, Inc.

Goldman, R., & Papson, S. (1998). *Nike Culture: The Sign of the Swoosh*. London: Sage Publications Ltd.

Hurley, R. F. (2006, September). The Decision to Trust. *Harvard Business Review* .

Kohn, A. (1999). *Punished by Rewards*. Boston: Houghton Mifflin.

Martinez, B., & Martinez, M. (1992). The Primacy of Principles. *The 10 Principles of Leaderhip Power* , 1.

Optimism = Sales Success: Metropolitan Life Case Study. (n.d.). Retrieved June 1, 2016, from MindResources. net: http://www.mindresources.net/marketing/website/profilingtools/MetLifeCaseStudyMRSSS.pdf

Pryce-Jones, J. (2010). *Happiness at Work*. West Sussex: Wiley-Blackwell.

Schulz, K. (2011, March). *On Being Wrong*. Retrieved June 1, 2016, from TED Ideas Worth Spreading: http://www.ted.com/talks/kathryn_schulz_on_being_wrong#t-227743

Segalla, M. (2009, June). How Europeans Do Layoffs. *Harvard Business Review* .

Sherman, L. (1996). *Popcorn King: How Orville Redenbacher and His Popcorn Charmed America*. Arlington: The Summit Publishing Group.

Simons, T. (2002, September). The High Cost of Low Trust. *Harvard Business Review* .

Stone, D., Patton, B., & Heen, S. (1999). *Difficult Conversations: How to Discuss What Matters Most*. New York: Penguin Books.

Training, D. C. (2012). *Enhancing Employee Engagement: The Role of the Immediate Manager*. New York: Dale Carnegie & Associates, Inc.

Wilkinson, K. (2011). *I Am Strong! The Formula to Build Your Self-Worth and Discover Your True Purpose from the Inside Out!* The Happiness Factor.

CPSIA information can be obtained
at www.ICGtesting.com
Printed in the USA
LVOW13s1608211216
518287LV00011B/1356/P